"Bedzow provides a compelling and practical framework for health care providers to act on their professional values. He goes beyond an analysis of actual cases to giving us the skills to speak up so we do the right thing for our patients. This is a book that anyone committed to creating an ethical culture of continuous improvement should read."

Lisa Soleymani Lehmann, MD, PhD,
Harvard Medical School and Veterans Health AdministrationAdministration

"In a remarkable confluence of scholarship and practical wisdom, Bedzow's short book manages to be academically rigorous but much more than an academic treatise. He has woven together several contemporary views of medical professionalism, along with the powerful vision of the Giving Voice to Values paradigm, to create a novel take on virtue ethics that will be of special value not only to medical students but to clinicians at every career stage."

Matthew K. Wynia, Director, Center for Bioethics and Humanities,
and Professor of Medicine, University of Colorado, USA

"In addressing values, Professor Bedzow has moved the discussion and the teaching of ethics in health care from theories and principles to practice. This book offers a toolbox for recognizing and managing conflicting ideas in medical ethics in order to achieve practical, patient focused solutions. In that regard, as well as others, it is highly innovative and critically important."

T. Forcht Dagi, Distinguished Scholar and Professor, The School of Medicine, Queen's University Belfast, Northern Ireland

Dr. Bedzow has identified one of the biggest challenges in clinical ethics education: narrowing the gap between theoretical and practical. This outstanding and thoughtful text empowers students and clinicians to fully understand, embrace, and practice their values, ultimately optimizing the care of patients in difficult ethical situations.

Megan K. Applewhite, John A. Balint, MD, Chair and Interim Director, Alden March Bioethics Institute, Albany Medical College, USA

"Ira Bedzow's innovative approach goes beyond traditional medical ethics to the personhood of patient and physician and the values of their relationship. He teaches not only moral decision-making but also strategies for effective moral action – essential skills for all healthcare professionals."

Elizabeth A. Rider, Department of Pediatrics,
Harvard Medical School Lead, USA

"Bedzow's book is a valuable resource for both medical students and educators. Clinically-relevant cases prepare students to communicate effectively and ethically when faced with challenging situations. It bridges the gap between traditional bioethics and communication programs. I highly recommend it!"

Heidi Waldron, Medical Educator and Curriculum Designer, School of Medicine Fremantle, The University of Notre Dame, Australia

"By offering strategies for acting appropriately under complex circumstances, this short text provides a promising method to augment conventional approaches to teaching ethics and professionalism to medical students so they will be better prepared for the realities of clinical practice."

Jeremy Sugarman, Harvey M. Meyerhoff Professor of Bioethics and Medicine, Johns Hopkins Berman Institute of Bioethics, USA

"I highly recommend this book as a guide for all physicians as they seek to remain true to the Hippocratic Oath throughout their professional lives. Dr Bedzow is a highly skilled and professional guide through the maze of ethical challenges we encounter."

James Block, Former President and Chief Executive Officer of Johns Hopkins Health System and the Johns Hopkins Hospital

GIVING VOICE TO VALUES AS A PROFESSIONAL PHYSICIAN

Giving Voice to Values as a Professional Physician provides students with the theoretical background and practical applications for acting on their values in situations of ethical conflict. It is the first medical ethics book that utilizes the Giving Voice to Values methodology to instruct students in medical ethics and professionalism.

In doing so, it shifts the focus of ethics education from intellectually examining ethical theories and conflicts to emphasizing moral action. Each section of the book explains how moral decision-making and action can be implemented in the healthcare arena. Medical ethics cases are provided throughout in order to assist students in giving voice to their values and developing skills for professional action. The Giving Voice to Values methodology, and the cases in this book, do not focus on the big questions of academic ethics, but rather on the ethics of the everyday, even if the challenges presented are difficult. In other words, the ethical questions students will have to face, in this book and in medical education and practice, are about how to interact with others, whether they be patients or colleagues, who might have different ethical positions.

The book provides a unique guide for professional identity formation and the teaching of ethics in medical schools.

Ira Bedzow is the Director of the Biomedical Ethics and Humanities Program at New York Medical College and Senior Scholar at the Aspen Center for Social Values. He is the author of numerous books, articles, and chapters on law, ethics, and social values.

GIVING VOICE TO VALUES

Series Editor: Mary C. Gentile

The *Giving Voice to Values* series is a collection of books on Business Ethics and Corporate Social Responsibility that brings a practical, solutions-oriented, skill-building approach to the salient questions of values-driven leadership.

Giving Voice to Values (GVV: www.GivingVoiceToValues.org) – the curriculum, the pedagogy and the research upon which it is based – was designed to transform the foundational assumptions upon which the teaching of business ethics is based, and importantly, to equip future business leaders to know not only what is right – but how to make it happen.

Giving Voice to Values in the Legal Profession
Carolyn Plump

Giving Voice to Values in Accounting
Tara J. Shawver and William F. Miller

Giving Voice to Values as a Professional Physician
Ira Bedzow

GIVING VOICE TO VALUES AS A PROFESSIONAL PHYSICIAN

An Introduction to Medical Ethics

Ira Bedzow

Routledge
Taylor & Francis Group
LONDON AND NEW YORK

First published 2019
by Routledge
2 Park Square, Milton Park, Abingdon, Oxon OX14 4RN

and by Routledge
52 Vanderbilt Avenue, New York, NY 10017

Routledge is an imprint of the Taylor & Francis Group, an informa business

British Library Cataloguing in Publication Data
A catalogue record for this book is available from the British Library

Library of Congress Cataloging-in-Publication Data
A catalog record has been requested for this book

ISBN: 978-1-138-35349-7 (hbk)
ISBN: 978-1-138-38834-5 (pbk)
ISBN: 978-0-429-42540-0 (ebk)

Typeset in Bembo
by Taylor & Francis Books

CONTENTS

List of tables ix
Acknowledgements x
Preface xi

1 Ethics, professionalism, and Giving Voice to Values 1

The uniqueness of professionalism education 6
Professionalism as a value not a competency 8
Giving Voice to Values 12
Starting assumptions to give voice to one's values 16

2 Making moral decisions 22

The gut reaction 26
Moral awareness: bias check 29
Conformity bias 30
Obedience to authority 32
Framing 34
Recognizing and prioritizing facts and values 35
The patient–physician relationship 36
Patient autonomy 37
Physicians' professional goals 37
Physician authority and professional integrity 37
One note on values 39
Ethical frameworks 39
Deontological (Kantian) ethics 41

Consequentialist (utilitarian) ethics 43
Value(s) comparison between deontology and consequentialism 45
Principlism or the Four Principles approach 47

3 Acting on moral decisions 50

Moral (inaction): Rationalizations check 50
Personal–professional profiles 51
Considering other stakeholders 53
Organizational and systems-based levers 54
Creating scripts 55

4 Cases 58

Case 1: Confronting a superior 57
Case 2: HIV mothers and breastfeeding their newborns 62
Case 3: Reporting a colleague 68
Case 4: Talking to family members about a patient's medical information 73
Case 5: Speaking to a colleague about a patient's complaints 76
Case 6: Complementary and alternative medicine 82
Case 7: Talking to patients about assisted reproductive technologies 87
Case 8: Withdrawing treatment and right to die 91
Case 9: Determination of death 95

5 Conclusion 101

Intended audience and how to use this book *103*
Example action plan and script for Case 1 *112*

TABLE

A1.1 Script and Action Plan Assessment Rubric 110

ACKNOWLEDGEMENTS

This book is a culmination of my trying to create a medical ethics course that helps students develop skills for acting ethically in life and in their future professional careers. It is also meant to give them the means by which they can identify with the values of the medical profession as they form their own professional identities. To that effect, I would like to thank the talented and thoughtful medical and interprofessional ethics faculty with whom I have worked at New York Medical College, who challenge me to think about how to improve the pedagogical methodology used in our courses. I would also like to thank the medical, dental, physical therapy, and speech pathology students who participated in the various ethics courses at New York Medical College that I directed, who allowed me to test different methods and formats and who provided valuable feedback so as to continually improve the quality of their ethics education. In particular, I would like to thank Pamela Ludmer, Noam Stadlan, Heidi Waldron, and Jeanne Wilson, who reviewed different chapters and cases in this book and contributed editorial insights. Of course, this book could not have been written without the support and mentoring of Mary Gentile. Mary is a gifted teacher who has permitted me to adapt her Giving Voice to Values philosophy to my own teaching and has pushed me to consider how best to incorporate her approach to medical ethics education. She truly demonstrates the value of leadership, in that she believes that the success of her students is a testament to the success of her teaching. And to my family – "Our tree of life is not guarded by cherubic swordsmen, but by the depth of our connection to each other."

PREFACE

I have taught courses in ethics to many different types of students and at different educational institutions, ranging from high school and undergraduate students, to seminarians and students pursuing careers in health care. While these courses in ethics were meant to teach students about moral values and ethical norms, they were also intended to help students act morally in the "real world" based on the assumption that by teaching students about ethics, they would learn to be ethical. These practical ethics courses typically ran as follows: After a brief introduction about a general ethical issue or principle, a hypothetical case would be presented which would highlight a moral question related to the topic of the session. The case would describe certain facts about the location, the community, and the relevant laws or regulations that could affect how any decision could be carried out. The case might even include multiple characters who either would be affected or must be incorporated into the decision that the students must make about how the case should be handled. However, oftentimes, the case itself would not be particularly relevant for the class discussion. The reason for the case's irrelevance would be because the class discussion would stay at the level of examining the moral question in and of itself, leaving the case as a simple example of how the question might play out in the world. Class discussion would seldom lead to imagining how one can act effectively in the given scenario based on the moral values and principles that the students held.

When students would discuss the pertinent moral question in ways that could lead to a decision on what they think should be done in the given case, both they themselves and the other participants in the discussion would approach suggestions by considering the limits of any proposal rather than its efficacy or consequences. This would lead the group to reject proposals through *reductio ad absurdum* or through making strained analogies before they could consider a proposal on its own merits. When discussion leads students to mention factors or views which other students did not consider, the group will try to shape their answers to incorporate different students' views, even when including those factors leads to contradictory reasoning. In this way, the class attempts to reach conclusions by consensus. Oftentimes, conclusion by consensus is not reached and students are left with more questions than answers. This unfortunate result is justified by teachers and students alike through the admission that ethics is difficult. Ethics is difficult, but that does not mean that students should be taught that answers to moral questions are out of reach for them.

Sometimes, a student (or a teacher) will push very strongly for a certain view, causing the other members of the class to agree reluctantly or to remain divisive. When this occurs, students conclude that ethics is either about power or is relative or both. While social interaction will always demand that people recognize views different from their own and that people appreciate that effective social action requires more than simply good will, students should not be led to believe that every view is equally correct or that only the most powerful have an ability to make decisions that affect others.

Rarely, there will be a situation where everyone in the class agrees to a general solution of what should be done in response to a pertinent moral question. Yet, even in such a situation, the discussion concludes with students thinking that their general answer is a "one size fits all" solution for whenever one encounters a case that embodies this moral question. This agreement of what is the right decision is deemed a satisfying result, and we hope that, with this general solution, our students will be prepared to act ethically in the world outside the classroom. But we would be sorely mistaken, since it is not enough in ethics to know what one should do generally. For ethical action – rather than simply ethical discussion – to be incorporated in students' lives, ethics education must be personal and relevant. Students must learn to consider, not only what they would do generally, but in particular, what words would they say in a given situation; what consequences can they foresee for themselves and the other stakeholders; whether they would be able to overcome reasons for not acting; whether they would be able to persuade those who disagree to follow their recommendation; and so on. While this is a problem for many different areas of ethical living, it is especially problematic in medical ethics education. Health care professionals must work and act in highly structured organizational settings alongside people who have different moral and professional goals and for the sake of patients who trust them even when they might disagree with them. Everyday healthcare professionals are challenged with practical ethical questions that need more than simply general notions of what is right; they need scenario-specific plans for how to act in practice.

The pedagogical premises underlying the standard ethics educational format is twofold: First, this format assumes that the real difficulty in ethics education is in understanding the main concepts and principles that should be used in critical moral thinking. As such, currently the real difference between theoretical ethics and practical ethics education is that in the former students evaluate the moral worth of the premises of different moral philosophies. Students of theoretical ethics try to answer questions such as "is rationality the ultimate test for ethical judgment?" or "is it more ethical to give priority to the greatest number over the greatest overall good?" Practical ethics takes these premises for granted and applies different moral frameworks to general questions that relate to contemporary topics, addressing questions like, "is it ethical to manipulate genes for the betterment of society?" or "would capping health care costs for end-of-life care result in increased wellbeing for members of society?" As one can see by these "practical" questions, however, students and professors alike can speak at length about these moral questions, but the answers to these practical ethics questions do not lead to acting ethically in practice, since seldom does this form of ethics education concern itself with devising effecting action plans for how to address these questions in the real world.

This leads to the second underlying pedagogical premise of the standard ethics educational format. We assume that carrying out individual ethical decisions are easy once someone decides what the right or good thing to do is. Barring questions that demand political or major organizational lobbying, in other words for everyday moral choices, all one has to do is act. Yet, for any other practical training, such as in business, law, and medicine, students are explicitly taught how to carry out decisions. Business students learn different strategies for implementing business decisions successfully. Law students learn not only whether a law suit is warranted but how to file one properly and argue one's position persuasively. Medical students learn not only whether a certain medical intervention is indicated or not, but also how actually to provide that treatment properly. In the same way, medical ethics education in particular, and ethics education in general, cannot assume that people will simply act ethically when they put their minds to it. Given the complexity of our social and professional worlds, ethical action must be taught with the same priority as any other practical training.

This book, and the Giving Voice to Values methodology that it uses, attempts to ameliorate the imbalance between thinking and acting in medical ethics education. The underlying premise of the book is that students desire to act on values that they already possess. The goal for medical ethics education, therefore, is to train them to be effective in doing so. This means learning how to think through and construct practical action strategies and communication scripts for the moral questions that the cases in this book present so that students develop skills of effective moral action for particular cases at hand. Students will learn both how to come to a decision that gives voice to their own values, which is informed by ethical reasoning and critical thinking, and how they can act on their decisions, given the complexity of the environment in which they must act. This practical ethics education works to show that moral thinking and acting are two sides to the same ethical lens, and students should continually look through both sides of that glass to get the best perspective.

1

ETHICS, PROFESSIONALISM, AND GIVING VOICE TO VALUES

Before the mid-nineteenth century, medical ethics was thought to be a personal ethics that was derived from a physician's understanding of his role, and its requisite duties, in society. Moral traits, or virtues, were delineated to characterize what constituted a good physician, and individuals endeavored on their own to develop good characters and uphold the values of the profession. For example, Benjamin Rush, a Founding Father of the United States and Surgeon General in the Continental Army, gave a lecture in 1801 entitled, "On the Vices and Virtues of Physicians," which described the moral virtues that are consistent with being a good physician and which vices physicians should avoid.

As the medical profession attempted to gain professional autonomy (which in this case means the autonomy of physicians as a group to self-regulate who could be admitted into the profession and not the autonomy of individual professionals to assert their own values), the view of what constituted proper professional practice changed from focusing on the personal development of individual physicians to creating a uniform set of norms to which all professionals should adhere. In 1847, in order to create such a standard that would be consistent for physicians, the American Medical Association (AMA) published its first Code of Ethics. In doing so, the AMA changed the practice of medicine from being based in personal moral character to being based on a standardized professional code of conduct. The code established a model which attempted to standardize ethical decisions for medical situations, giving professional consensus moral authority over any person's individual conscience. As such, the AMA Code took primacy over a physician's personal, religious, or moral beliefs and values in an attempt to bolster the authority of the profession. (Though, the current AMA code does allow for conscientious objection when a certain practice goes against a physician's personal, religious, or moral beliefs.) This transition changed how professionals viewed medical ethics, since under the authority of the Code, questions of medical ethics were reframed in terms of what to do in a situation and not necessarily which values one should adopt and convey as a physician.

While today, most if not all health care professions and specialties have codes of ethics specific to them, there has been increasing emphasis on explicit instruction and adoption of professional values and the development of professional (or moral) character traits. This emphasis is relatively new in medicine. The term "professionalism" as a way to connote humanistic and moral values, such as altruism, duty and service, accountability, and excellence, only started to be used in the 1990s, though the concept began to take shape in the mid-1980s.[1] This is not to say that before the 1980s physicians did not try to develop personal moral values and apply them in their medical practices. Many doctors did just that, but as part of their own moral development and growth. Today, however, there is a push to formalize professionalism as an educational competency and a priority for clinical practice.

The importance of professionalism in the current health care environment cannot be stressed enough, and explicit instruction geared towards the development of proper professional habits must come early and must be reinforced often. Quality of care is becoming a greater priority, medical technology is becoming more and more sophisticated, and society is becoming more culturally and religiously diverse, leading to tensions between values among stakeholders. As such, professionalism has become a greater part of one's educational and employment responsibilities than ever before.

Because recognition of the importance of professionalism is widespread, professionalism has become a required competency in undergraduate and in graduate medical education. All medical schools across the country are attempting to introduce the subject into their curricula both longitudinally across the four years of medical school and horizontally among different courses and clerkships. Given the relationship between medical ethics and professionalism, most professionalism training begins with courses in medical ethics during the preclinical portion of the curriculum, which is then reinforced in practice during students' clinical rotations. Yet, the scholarly literature shows that there is actually an erosion of professionalism and humanism among medical students and residents as they proceed through their education.[2] This phenomenon is not due to a lack of awareness, since the need to develop ways to nurture medical students' compassion is well recognized, nor is it a result of a lack of available resources. Rather, it is due, in part, to the inability to provide a means to combine the teaching of ethical theories and professionalism concepts with skills and tools for habit formation that can be demonstrated through observable behaviors. As David Thomas Stern has noted, "While educators have made great strides over the past 50 years in assessing knowledge, and over at least the past 20 years in assessing skills, the assessment of behaviors and professionalism has lagged."[3] Instruction of professional skills and the inculcation of professional habits is more difficult than teaching clinical knowledge and training students to develop proper clinical skills and behaviors, since professionalism also includes an affective component, where students' attitudes and motivations toward adopting those behaviors include personal identification with the values those behaviors express. What has ultimately been lacking, therefore, is a truly transformational approach to professionalism education, in which the focus is not just on knowledge acquisition, but also on affective and behavioral change.

Currently, early medical ethics education consists of teaching students ethical terms and theories, as well as professional codes and rules regarding different aspects of medical practice, so that students can understand the general ideas behind ethical controversies or challenges that they may face in clinical practice. The pedagogical assumption behind this method of ethics instruction is based in Lawrence Kohlberg's cognitivist theory of moral development. While Kohlberg's theory primarily relates to the moral development of children, it is applied to the ethical and professional development of students in the following way: When they enter the professional community, students are still at the pre-conventional reasoning level, where they perceive professional and medical ethics challenges from their own egocentric frame, reasoning through cases from their own perspectives and experiences. Through giving students professional codes and laws, and by having students talk about ethical cases, students will reach the conventional reasoning level, where they learn to recognize and apply the social conventions of the profession. When they enter the clinical stage of their education, students will obey social rules but are also expected to learn how to apply moral principles to particular situations, recognizing the nuances of their experiences. In this post-conventional level, their professionality and ethical habits will be based in their ethical thinking rather than considering what to do situationally or through simply imitating their teachers and colleagues. In the Kohlbergian methodology, moral action stems directly from moral thinking. If a person is able to determine the right course of action, he or she will automatically follow it. Also, Kohlberg assumed that once a person reaches a higher level of moral reasoning, he or she will apply it uniformly across different situations and will not slide backwards to lower stages.

While there is much to the Kohlbergian model for medical ethics education, it has been challenged by empirical studies that have tested the behavior of students in their clerkship years. For example, Hegazi and Wilson assessed moral judgment competence in 880 medical students in Sydney, Australia, over two different studies to determine whether moral development occurs during medical school or not.[4] Participants completed Lind's Moral Judgment Test, which is based on Kohlberg's stages of moral development. They found that students did not apply moral principles consistently over different contexts. Rather, students decreased in moral judgment competence with respect to applying ethical principles to medical scenarios but remained at the same level of competence for non-medical scenarios.[5] Similarly, Feitosa et al., observed regression of moral judgment competence in medical students in Brazil, and stagnation, with a tendency to regression, of moral judgment competence for medical students in Portugal from the first semester to their eighth semester of medical school.[6] Also, Slováčková, and Ladislav observed a significant decrease in moral judgment competence for 310 Czech and Slovak and 70 foreign national students at the Medical Faculty of Charles University in the Czech Republic.[7]

This disconnect in terms of what students are learning in their preclerkship ethics courses and how they are acting during their clerkships raises questions about the existence of a "hidden curriculum," where students are learning unprofessional and unethical social conventions through observing how faculty and residents behave. The regression is explained by positing that these conventions have a much stronger influence on students' professional identity, since they perceive these behaviors as the actual conventions to obey rather than identifying with the overt instruction that they receive in the classroom. The notion that students learn professional and ethical behavior through their environment, rather than through direct instruction of ethical theory, is supported by John Haidt's social intuitionist theory of moral action.

Haidt's Social Intuitionist Model advances the idea that moral reasoning is subsequent to an automatic process, where decisions are made quickly, effortlessly, and unconsciously, rather than being intentional and effortful, and only after a decision is made does the person think about the ethics of it.[8] In other words, moral reasoning serves to give rationalizations for conclusions rather than giving reasons for them. Haidt's theory holds that there are five sets of intuitions that ground morality, namely, harm/care, fairness/reciprocity, authority/respect, purity/sanctity, and in-group/out-group.[9] Moral development occurs through a process whereby the five moral intuition sets interact with an external social environment that promotes particular values. As opposed to the Kohlbergian view that moral development is being hindered by an immoral hidden curriculum, in this model, moral development is a consequence of how one's environment interacts with a person's moral intuitions. In other words, one theory's hidden curriculum is the other theory's situational influences. The difference between the two terms is that in the Kohlbergian approach, the "morally inappropriate" environment interferes with student's moral development, whereas in Haidt's theory, the environment inculcates different moral values that students learn as part of their moral development.[10] Therefore, under Haidt's interpretative scheme, the medical students in the above studies do not demonstrate moral regression or segmentation; rather, their moral judgment did develop, albeit according to the values presented in their new environment.

If Haidt's Social Intuitionist Model is correct, then a Kohlbergian approach, where educators provide a stronger foundation in moral theory to students in medical ethics classes would not be effective in creating humanistic professionals. What is required is a change of culture in hospitals so that medical students' intuitions develop through exposure to the professional culture that we want to exist rather than the one that exists at present. Any education in moral theory would only provide justification after-the-fact for choices made; it would not inculcate medical ethics thinking or professionalism in an environment where it does not exist already.

These finding are not particular to medical ethics education. In the book, *Lost in Transition: The Dark Side of Emerging Adulthood*, [11] the authors discuss the results of interviews they conducted with 230 young adults to determine what issues were facing America's youth. Based on their interviews, the team saw that the way in which young adults thought about ethical questions in the abstract did not relate to the way they actually acted in situations where they could have implemented their abstract thinking. The interviewees were able to answer questions concerning extreme cases of right and wrong, implying that they were able to think about morality and make moral decisions. Yet, when asked about their own personal lives, they did not rely on any moral reasoning when answering even basic questions. Rather, they deferred to how they felt or how they regularly acted in those types of situations.

This example seems to support Haidt's social intuitionist theory, yet there is a different explanation which can account for why people revert to personal experiences to justify their actions yet still use moral thinking when considering abstract cases. It can also explain the change in moral judgment competence of students when faced with medical scenarios but not nonmedical scenarios. This alternative explanation allows for Kohlbergian prescriptivity, in that there is a definite trajectory of moral development that medical ethics and professionalism should promote, while accepting Haidt's descriptive observations of how one's social environment influences a person's moral development.[12] The disconnect between students' ability to reason in abstract and their inability to apply ethical thinking to their own lives should be understood in terms of what is called the moral gap between thinking and acting. Living ethically is about both moral thinking and moral action – the two are distinct, with different skills needed to do either well. Having one set of skills does not necessarily entail that you have the other. In order to come up with a moral decision and to act on it, people must think about how to evaluate different moral choices, as well as the personal and situational factors that affect which choices one can implement. Coming up with the right answer of "what should be done" does not easily translate to the right answer of "what I can do." When students deliberate on "what should be done," they may reach an answer that they do not know how to implement or are unable to implement, given their practical knowledge, personal strengths and weaknesses, or their role in the group that faces the moral challenge. When "what should be done" conflicts with "what I can do," students will revert to answering the question "what I can do" based on what they have seen done or have done in the past. It is not that students cannot come up with moral decisions; it is that they cannot conceive of a plan to enact them and give voice to their values. However, if students are trained to imagine how they can act in a way that aligns with their values in different situations and can practice doing so, they will be able to develop skills and "moral muscle memory" to make it easier to do so in the future. In a sense, they will be learning how intellectual moral competence (the Kohlbergian approach) can be complemented by awareness of the social-intuitionist approach so that students are able to expand their view of what is possible and "re-wire" instinctive, emotional responses. This will make values-driven action more likely, since they will be aware of the environmental challenges and opportunities that may be present and have tools to act in that environment, rather than simply knowing what should be done without knowing how to do it – or worse, simply accepting inaction out of a sense of inefficacy.

The uniqueness of professionalism education

Professionalism education is particularly challenging because unlike other medical education competencies, the objective criteria for demonstrating professionalism is not clear cut in terms of providing operational definitions. Many definitions for professionalism can be found, from short descriptions, such as:

> Medical professionalism is a belief system in which group members ("professionals") declare ("profess") to each other and the public the shared competency standards and ethical values they promise to uphold in their work and what the public and individual patients can and should expect from medical professionals,[13]

to longer definitions, such as the one laid out in the Physician Charter, authored by the ABIM Foundation (American Board of Internal Medicine), in conjunction with the ACP Foundation (American College of Physicians) and the European Federation of Internal Medicine, which includes a definition, fundamental principles, and professional responsibilities.[14] Despite the numerous definitions (and attempts to assess student professionalism), however, most faculty and students rely on intuition rather than objectivity, and adapt Justice Potter Stewart's definition for pornography ("I know it when I see it"), thereby relegating professionalism to a category that is subjective and lacking of clearly defined parameters.

While the requirements for any assessed competency in medical education should be clear, complete and concise, with multiple opportunities for students to be observed, evaluated, and given feedback, professionalism as a competency currently has no standard either for instruction or assessment. This is because professionalism is unique in two respects. First, professionalism is not strictly a matter of knowing content or performing certain behaviors. It entails identifying with certain beliefs, principles, and values, is associated with having certain attitudes towards those beliefs, principles, and values, and is manifest in certain behaviors. While behavior can be observed and assessed, such as measuring a person's communication skills, attitudes and beliefs can be inferred only indirectly. Medical educators are consistently frustrated by the inability to quantify and assess beliefs and values such as compassion, empathy, and genuine caring for patients. Moreover, because professionalism is an internal motivation for feeling and acting a certain way, once people know that they are being observed and assessed, there will always be ambiguity as to whether those being observed are acting through the intrinsic motivation of professionalism or in order to be assessed positively.

Second, while there are general modes of behavior associated with professionalism, how professionalism will be expressed is environment-dependent. Professional behavior must account for a variability of factors in the healthcare environment, such as with whom one works, the types of patients one sees, the types of illnesses one treats, and the financial arrangements that influence how the health system operates. For example, one recognized component of sustaining professionalism is to improve access to care. This is an ideal to which everyone can agree is a value of professional practice, yet its implementation is not wholly dependent on any one individual. Improving access to care demands cooperation between those who control healthcare resources, public health leaders, insurance companies, and patients. How any individual can uphold the value of improving access to care must therefore depend, not only on his or her aspiration to do so, but also on his or her ability to do so given his or her relationships to those other factors that determine access. If a person has the belief that this value is important, but is limited in his or her means to effectuate it, then it becomes a very difficult component of professionalism to assess. Furthermore, many medical schools do not have formal instruction to teach how any individual can improve access to care. As such, students are being assessed on (part of) a competency for which they are not being instructed on how to attain it.

Moreover, moral and professional challenges arise in particularities and not in generalities. Each challenge stems from the personal values, backgrounds, capabilities and limitations of the particular medical student trying to act on his or her values, as well as those of the other stakeholders in the situation. The uniqueness of each individual plays a major part in establishing the learning objectives of the experience for the sake of teaching and assessing professionalism. While it may be possible to provide students with opportunities to develop their professional identities and increase their abilities to act on their values, professionalism education must be seen in a much more individualized light than other competencies.

Another issue that affects professionalism today is the fact that the healthcare system is very different than it was a generation ago. The patient–physician relationship has changed from being paternalistic, where the doctor was the one who directed the course of treatment, to one that maintains a priority of patient autonomy and shared decision-making between doctor and patient. This can be seen not only from the big-picture changes in the way healthcare is delivered, but even in the everyday complaints and compliments one hears when people talk about their visits to the doctor. Patients and family members are more attuned to whether their physicians are rude or sensitive, impatient or attentive, than whether they demonstrate proficiency of medical knowledge and clinical skills. This is partly because they are not aware of how to gauge medical competence, yet the primary reason is because as much as patients want their diseases to be treated, they expect that their doctors will empathize with their illness experiences and respect their involvement in choosing a treatment plan.[15] This change in the patient–physician relationship means that what constitutes professional behavior has changed. Old models of professionalism training may no longer be applicable in this new environment, which emphasizes different values.

In addition to the change in nature of the patient–physician relationship, healthcare has also become much more interprofessional and collaborative, where physicians are members of a team and not always the leader of that team. Furthermore, many physicians are now more often employed by hospitals and healthcare systems rather than having their own practices. All of these changes to the nature of the profession have impacted the nature of professionalism. Even if many of the values of professionalism remain intact, previous models of professional practice are less applicable in today's current healthcare environment, leaving new initiates into the profession with less guidance from mentors who have not yet acclimated to the changing culture.

Professionalism as a value not a competency

Rather than viewing professionalism simply as an educational competency to be achieved and assessed, professionalism education would be more productive when taught through the lens of virtue ethics, where professionalism is seen as a value that demands that people attain certain competencies in order to express that value well, and where students develop those competencies and identify with professionalism as a value through the moral pedagogy that virtue ethics puts forth. Virtue ethics, as a theory of moral growth and character development, emphasizes the idea that personal virtues, or a person's character, changes over time and, with proper intellectual and behavioral instruction, people can improve with respect to identifying with, and acting on, moral values. The theory approaches ethics longitudinally rather than looking just at individual actions. It is a much more complicated ethical framework to describe than other moral philosophies, such as deontology or consequentialism, when applied in practice, since it does not use a moral formula or maxim to judge whether a person should act one way or another. Instead, it asks us to think about the values that we aspire to demonstrate through our habits and how we can demonstrate them effectively in different situations. It also asks us to think "What type of person would I be if I made a habit out of one thing or another?" More generally, it assumes that we know which values are proper to uphold and which traits are good to acquire, either through our own moral inclinations or because our society or community has imparted them to us. In both professionalism literature and virtue ethics, a group of people, such as a community or a profession, advocates for certain ideals to be accepted and, much of the time, professionalism – like virtue – is not explicitly defined but people generally know what is expected. Moreover, acculturation into a profession comes through experience, whether that experience is through mentoring and imitating those who behave in ways to which one aspires, or through recognizing unprofessional behaviors and avoiding or challenging those who act that way. Without proper attention, any hidden curriculum or social environment can be quite damaging for the development of character or appropriate professional traits, yet when people and organizations are mindful both of what the ideal is and how one can gain the tools and habits to achieve it, then a virtue ethics pedagogy is a more encompassing process than learning to apply moral formulations or simple behavioral competencies to every situation.

In applying a virtue ethics framework, professionalism should be seen as a meta-value, which is a value that encompasses other values.[16] Oftentimes, moral challenges occur when a person has to find a balance between conflicting values that he or she holds. Professionalism as a meta-value would mean that the person aspires to find the best prioritization for conflicting values that affect decision-making and action in a given situation so as to behave in the way that maximizes his or her demonstration of all held values. When seen as a meta-value, we can rely on conceptions of integrity in the ethical literature to understand and apply professionalism to medical education and practice. Reliance on the conception of integrity is in line with the description of professionalism, found in the Physician Charter mentioned above, as the basis of medicine's contract with society, which states, "Essential to [professionalism] is public trust in physicians, which depends on the integrity of both individual physicians and the whole profession."[17] Gabriel Taylor defines integrity as being sincerely true to one's commitments and having the fortitude of will to stay committed to them. The person of integrity "will be rational in a number of related ways. He will not ignore relevant evidence, he will be consistent in his behaviour, he will not act on reasons which, given the circumstances, are insufficient reasons for action."[18] Similarly, Lynne McFall defines integrity as the state of being undivided or as an integral whole. This entails having consistency within one's set of principles or commitments and having coherence between one's principles, actions, and the motivations behind them.[19] Just as integrity entails being true to one's commitments, so can professionalism be conceived of as being true to, adhering to, and identifying with, the medical competencies that define the medical profession. For a virtue ethics analogy, the professional not only knows how to act properly and does act properly in given situations but he or she also wants to act that way because he or she fully identifies with those actions as a demonstration of his or her values. The distinction we can make between the competent physician versus the professional physician is similar to Aristotle's distinction between the "good person" and the "noble-and-good person," where the former just accepts the importance of acting properly while the latter is reflective about goodness and finds it praiseworthy in and of itself.

Conceptualizing professionalism as a meta-value rather than simply as an educational competency allows medical educators to distinguish between competent behaviors and students' aspirations to be professionals. Otherwise, if we keep thinking about professionalism simply as another educational competency, it subsumes or permeates into all the other medical school educational competencies. This either creates ambiguity as to what professionalism actually is or it leads to giving professionalism a nod while, at the same time, dismissing it, since it has no actual objectives or milestones that are different from the other educational competencies. For example, besides professionalism, other major medical school educational competencies are "patient care," "medical knowledge," "interpersonal communication and communication skills," "interprofessional collaboration," "practice-based learning and improvement," and "systems-based practice." Subcompetencies that are associated with professionalism are:

1. demonstrate responsiveness to patient needs,
2. demonstrate respect for patient privacy and autonomy,
3. demonstrate honesty, integrity, and trustworthiness with patients, documentation, family members, and colleagues,
4. relate to others with respect, care, and compassion,
5. respond to colleagues' needs, expectations, and concerns,
6. demonstrate responsibility, leadership, and accountability,
7. demonstrate excellence and scholarship, and
8. demonstrate a commitment to ethical policies and compliance with relevant laws, policies, and regulations.

When looking at the list of subcompetencies, it becomes obvious that subcompetencies 1–3 can be seen as part of "patient care," subcompetencies 3–6 can be seen as part of "interprofessional collaboration" and "interpersonal communication and communication skills," subcompetency 7 can apply to "medical knowledge" and "practice-based learning and improvement," and subcompetency 8 applies to "systems-based practice." Thus, while treating professionalism as a separate competency, we have set its parameters in terms of the other competencies and have not framed professionalism as the means to encourage the development of ethical physicians who will strive to continually improve their abilities to act on their personal and professional values.

Those who see professionalism as a value that demands that people attain certain competencies in order to express that value well rather than as an educational competency in and of itself will continually endeavor to make professionalism part of their identity and behavior, since it is not simply a set of skills that a person can master. This reframing can therefore serve as motivation for life-long and self-directed learning, since its application will never be routine. Moreover, viewing professionalism as a value recognizes that it is an aspect of all other clinical competencies without reducing it to a set of behaviors. This addresses the challenges that professionalism has in the realm of education and assessment, namely, if it can't be measured objectively, then it can't be assessed, and students don't learn what faculty expect but rather what they assess.[20] From the perspective of students, when professionalism is spoken of as an educational competency that is similar to the others, yet its instruction and assessment are not analogous, they perceive professionalism as less important than the other competencies. From the perspective of the educators, to mitigate the difficulty of teaching professionalism as a competency, medical education has sought to reduce this burden by expecting students to possess it before they come to medical school, as demonstrated by the rise in admission interviews which ask students to answer social and ethical questions as part of the admissions process. Furthermore, while there are components in medical school, such as the Gold Humanism Honor Society, which recognize when students and faculty serve as role models, major discussions regarding how to teach professionalism often occur when students fail to exhibit it.

If we are to take the similarities between professionalism education and virtue ethics seriously, then we should consider the premise which Aristotle grounds his theory of moral development. Aristotle begins with the assumption that his students have had a proper moral upbringing, by which he means that they already have a good idea as to the proper values with which they should aspire to identify and the types of behaviors which will put those values into action.[21] The purpose of Aristotle's moral pedagogy is for his students to develop intellectually and morally, cultivating their moral characters so that they become second-nature. Similarly, most students who enter medical school do so because they want to help people. They also have a good idea as to the values and conceptions they should aspire to uphold in caring for people through their experiences as family members and friends, both in terms of helping and being helped by others. Professionalism education, like moral pedagogy in virtue ethics, should first and foremost provide students with a means to develop their own professional characters by relying on the values to which they already want to give voice. In this way, education is a means of self-refinement, both intellectually and habitually, and not solely a means of imparting new content and skills. Pedagogically, professionalism is to be learned and not taught.

To demonstrate what I mean, consider the pedagogical tool of having students learn through self-recognition. This is particularly important when uncovering certain biases that students may have which limit their ability to care for patients and apply already-held values. For example, despite identifying with the general value of wanting to care for and treat patients, there are many situations where a student might perceive that patients are responsible for their conditions or are simply very difficult to engage, and a student may therefore be less motivated to help them. Instead of directly instructing students to care, a more productive strategy would be to expose (1) why they might have their negative perception, and (2) how they might change that perception so as to better act on their values. One way to do this would be to reveal students' attribution biases.[22] When a patient's disposition or character is seen to have caused his or her condition, the physician might be less empathetic to his or her plight than if it is seen as a product of circumstance. In making students aware of their attributional assumptions and facilitating their recognition of potential situational factors that might be influencing their patients' behavior and health, they can learn on their own how to act on their primary value of wanting to care for patients, regardless of the situation. The same is true in understanding how to create better working relationships between different members of a healthcare team.

The same pedagogical technique can be used to help students understand the values behind a healthcare law or hospital policy. For example, when students attribute an incorrect understanding for why certain policies or guidelines are in place, they are more likely to ignore them, especially when the consequences for doing so are minimal or inconsistent. This does not end upon graduation; clinicians who have a negative perception of clinical guidelines will also be less compliant. To change this perception, it is not enough to inform people of the guideline's purpose; consistent compliance demands internalization and identification. The process of learning how to accept, internalize, and identify with institutional guidelines can be taught by asking students what their current conception of the guideline is, what assumptions did they make that lead to that conception, and how can they adopt a more positive understanding of the policy. This is not to say that all hospital policies are correct, but it does allow students who disagree with a policy to understand how best to respond to the policy's position in a way that is more efficacious than simply noncompliance.

Understanding professionalism education as a means to provide opportunities for students to improve upon what they already want to achieve allows the development of professionalism to be intrinsically motivated, even when students learn to conform to the medical profession's ethos and norms. The voluntary nature of their motivation allows students to search for and examine the values which are laden in the laws, ethics codes, policies, and formal instruction so as to make them their own. Their adoption and incorporation are not coercive, in terms of students acting in accordance with them because they have to; rather, they are seen as part of the processes of self-improvement, given their professional and personal goals. Moreover, as students develop professionally, they will not compartmentalize their professional experiences and their personal ones, since they will see their professional experiences as part of who they are.

In incorporating professionalism education through a virtue ethics frame, the educational format should be that professionalism is conceived of a meta-value that consists of values that students already uphold as well as values inherent to the medical profession. Students should also appreciate that in order to express the value of professionalism, and the different values that it encompasses, they need to attain certain behavioral competencies which become second-nature through the development of habits. Pedagogy should be consistent with a humanistic theory of learning, where development of the student encompasses cognitive, affective, and behavioral needs so that students can develop on their own. The curriculum should provide opportunities for students to desire intrinsically to act on their values as faculty give them guidance on how to act on them successfully. Educators should recognize the difference between values and competencies, in terms of what we can impart as knowledge and assess as skills. The professionalism question that students should continually strive to answer is – "*What if you were going to act on your values – what would you say and do?*" This question is the basis of the Giving Voice to Values methodology, which will be discussed in the next section.

Giving Voice to Values

Giving Voice to Values (GVV), which was created as an applied approach to business ethics, has become a valuable methodology to teach applied ethics in many different professions, because it shifts the focus of ethics education from intellectually examining ethical theories and conflicts to emphasizing moral action given one's commitment to moral values. This is not to say that the intellectual aspects of moral decision-making are not important, only that focusing on the development of knowledge of ethical theories does not necessitate the development of skills and practical know-how for successful moral action. On the other hand, a focus on moral action does necessitate the development of ethical knowledge, in the same way that virtue ethics supposes that habit formation corresponds with the development of practical reasoning. In other words, gaining experience in how to act on one's values and thinking about the best ways to act on them reinforces those values and allows a person to gain a deeper appreciation of those values as a consequence. GVV cases, therefore, do not simply ask, "What would you do in this situation?" Rather, it asks the following "Thought Experiment" – "What if you wanted to enact your values? What might you say or do?" In thinking about past cases, it asks, "Do you think that you would have been more confident and more effective in voicing your concerns if you had rehearsed ahead of time?" These questions presuppose that the person knows what he or she believes is right and that he or she wants to act on those beliefs. They ask the person to imagine ethical action as a training activity, where he or she can develop the competencies needed to express his or her values efficaciously. As such, it aligns with the notion that professionalism is a value that demands certain competencies to demonstrate one's appreciation of it. Furthermore, by asking a person these types of questions, the person gains a sense that there is a possible way forward in responding to ethical challenges. The frame shift is from whether one can act to how one could best act.[23]

In the GVV methodology, perceiving professional and medical ethics challenges from one's own egocentric frame and reasoning through cases from one's own perspective and experiences is not something that one should abandon as one develops, as it is in Kohlberg's theory of moral development. Yet, it is also not the complete story either. In the GVV methodology, one starts with the assumption that one's own perspective has moral cogency and is beneficial for finding the best way to respond, since the person must choose a path of action that fits with his or her own sense of self. However, the GVV methodology also recognizes that moral challenges require people to grasp the nuances and the influences of the social environment in which they must act, which includes appreciating social conventions that might help or hinder the success of their actions. In the end, the GVV approach aligns with Kohlberg in wanting people to learn how to act on their own moral values rather than react based on the situation or by simply imitating teachers and colleagues. The difference between Kohlberg's approach and the GVV approach is in that the former, development entails a change in the person's sense of self, while in the latter development entails building on one's sense of self.

Therefore, even though GVV is primarily a "post-decision" approach, it can be expanded to include improving ethical decision-making as well. This also fits with the idea that what one can do informs what one should do in a situation. It forces students to think of their values in action rather than as abstract principles to apply indiscriminately after affirming them. In other words, while recognizing what one values is a first step, GVV demands that one also thinks about how one's values can be applied successfully, given what the situation demands and one's personal capabilities in applying them.

In responding to an ethical challenge, there are generally three main approaches one could take. The "preaching stance" is when a person tries to counter opposing arguments or one's own personal temptations so that one will act morally. An example of this is when a person says (to himself or herself), "It is wrong to do X. Instead, I should do Y because it is the right thing to do." The "persuasive stance" is when a person does not counter opposing arguments or temptations directly but rather provides alternative reasons why acting ethically is a better option in practice. An example of this is when a person says (to himself or herself), "I understand why I might want to do X. But I will achieve what I want easier if I do Y instead." The "enabling stance" is when a person wants to act in accord with his or her values because he or she has those values and not for ulterior motives. It begins with deliberating on how to do so rather than on whether to do so. For example, the person says, "I choose to uphold the values and reasons to act in accord with my values. How can I best accomplish that?" Giving Voice to Values (GVV) adopts the "enabling stance" and is a teaching method that recognizes that teaching ethical analysis is not sufficient for creating ethical habits and professionalism. Therefore, the methodology of GVV asks students not to ask "what should be done" in an ethical challenge but rather what they can do to make sure that they advocate for what they believe is right. Of course, in medical ethics, one might not know immediately what the best choice might be; therefore, this book will also include instruction on how to reason towards a decision as part of the decision-making processes. However, reasoning to find what one wants to do in order to act on his or her values is only the first part; unlike the "preaching stance" or "persuasive stance," the "enabling stance" does not end there. The "enabling stance" ends in action, or at least for the purpose of the cases in this book, coming up with a script or strategy for effective action.

The question "*How can I best give voice to my values?*" is partly reflective of the ethical idea that "ought implies can" but it should not be seen in its traditional sense. Traditionally, the idea that "ought implies can" means that if I am to be truly moral I should be able to overcome any weakness that I might have to perform the right action simply because it is right. This demands too much without giving tools to overcome difficulties, nor does it recognize that moral action is a skill like any other and requires practice. Rather, the statement should be understood to mean that not only should I think about what I ought to do, I also need to think about what I can do in this situation, and that the former will enable me to fulfill the latter. The moral duty for a first year medical student would be different from a resident or from a teenager, since the abilities of each would be different. This way of understanding the idea that "ought implies can" says a lot about moral empowerment. If you know that you should act in a certain way and that you can act in a certain way, then you don't really have the excuse to say "well, this should be done, but I am not in a position to do it." Rather, you should say, "I know I ought, and I know I can, act in a way that I believe is right." It also gives a person the opportunity to recognize his or her own abilities and weaknesses to inform how to act to do what is right. What makes it even easier under a GVV methodology to enact this version of the idea that "ought implies can" is that the motivation behind doing what you think you ought to do is your desire to do just that. It is not an external ought that is imposed upon the person. Otherwise, we may be falling into a preaching stance rather than an enabling stance.

The GVV methodology, and the cases in this book, do not focus on the big questions of academic ethics, but rather on the ethics of the everyday, even if the challenges presented are difficult. In other words, the ethical questions students will have to face, both in this book and in medical education and practice more generally, are about how to interact with others, whether they be patients or colleagues, who might have different ethical positions. Yet, knowing your position on a given ethical issue will inform how you might interact with others to achieve what you want. In other words, the question in professional ethics in health care is not simply, "What is my position on a certain medical treatment or therapy?" Rather, it is, "How can I provide the best care to my patient and work most effectively with my colleagues in a way that I can maintain my own ethical integrity while respecting the people for whom I have a duty to care and with whom I work?"

If medical ethics education simply teaches how to employ different ethical frameworks to justify a solution, then students run the risk of learning how to manipulate ethical reasoning methods to support his or her own gut reactions or unreflective responses. This leaves students thinking that ethics is relative and that any answer is justifiable as long as one can find a persuasive means to justify it. However, if students do not learn how different ethical theories frame questions in order to reason to proper conclusions, they may be left without the ability to explain why their decisions have merit. This latter phenomenon is called "moral dumbfounding" and it creates a situation where people cannot give voice to their values, since they do not have the tools to express why their decision has value in the first place. As such, the GVV methodology should be seen as a corrective complement to the standard medical ethics instruction which focuses primarily on moral analysis, since, in order to act on one's values, one must also be able to think about them and how they apply to a given ethical challenge. It is designed to help students recognize which values they want to uphold, clarify how those values can be applied in a given case, and develop strategies and scripts to act on those values in successful ways. It recognizes that there might be situations where a person cannot uphold his or her values in the most optimal way, but even in these cases ethical decisions and actions should not be abandoned. Rather, the methodology provides a way for students to optimize their professionalism given the circumstance's opportunities and limitations, so that they do not perceive professionalism and professional behavior as all-or-nothing. As students improve in their abilities to act on their values, their confidence to do so will also increase. Confidence will be built both through their reliance on the scripts that they create and through their experience in being successful.

The goal of each case in this book is for students to have a means to practice their moral thinking and acting skills by ultimately creating scripts and strategies about how they would respond to the challenges of a given situation. In creating their strategies and scripts, students are forced to consider how decisions of what should be done in a given case proceeds from thinking about what they want and can do to enact those decisions. They will also learn to consider what they would actually say to the relevant parties in the scenario, to anticipate how others in the scenario might respond, and how they could continue the conversation to give voice to the values of their decision and persuade others to take their decision seriously. The purpose of this pedagogy is to reduce the number of times people act unethically, not because they want to act badly, but because they don't see how they can act in a different way. Mary Gentile, the founder of the GVV methodology, explains the pedagogy as follows:

> The thesis here is that if enough of us felt empowered – and were skillful and practiced enough – to voice and act on our values effectively on those occasions when our best selves are in the driver's seat, business would be a different place. In other words, this book is not about changing who we are, but rather it is about empowering the parts of us that already want to do the right thing.[24]

Professor Gentile's goal for business ethics should be ours for medical ethics and professionalism. In going through this process multiple times, students will be able to practice giving voice to their values, thereby building habits and skills in order to make it easier for them to do so when they face actual situations throughout their education and future careers.

Because the GVV methodology is meant to provide a means for students to become empowered to act, the cases that will be presented in this book will include not only a question regarding medical ethics but they will also include challenges that the student must consider when attempting to give voice to his or her values. External pressure might be from faculty that may not want to include the student as part of the health care team, a patient or family member that is demanding an outcome that conflicts with the student's values, or difficulties – whether they be organizational or personal – in communicating or working with different members of the collaborative care team. This external pressure will demand that students consider how to raise concerns; not only what concerns might need to be raised. By having students repeatedly engaging in creating practical and effective strategies for action, rehearsing how they would communicate with various stakeholders in the respective cases, and participating in peer discussion and coaching on how to improve, students will develop their skills and "moral muscle memory" for the challenges they will face. This is not only an important component of the GVV methodology, but it is also an important part of professional identity formation.

Starting assumptions to give voice to one's values

The Giving Voice to Values methodology presumes certain assumptions, which, when made explicit, make applying the methodology easier. The assumptions below are adapted from the twelve assumptions found in Mary Gentile's book, *Giving Voice to Values*.

First, a person wants to voice and act on his or her values. It leads to better decisions, and although one may not succeed, voicing one's values is worth doing. Ethical action will not occur if a person does not want to uphold the values that he or she has. Moreover, if a person has values but consistently chooses not to voice and act on them, then his or her actions demonstrate more clearly a lack of values than an identification with them. By making this assumption explicit, even if it might be obvious, it allows a person to hold himself or herself accountable for what he or she actually wants. The decision whether to act on one's values or not is now a choice to do what one wants to do rather than a question of obeying what one thinks one should do. This frame shift makes it easier for a person to act, since it is a matter of doing what the person is already intrinsically motivated to do.

When it comes to voicing and acting on your values, some of those values may be ones that you have held for a very long time. They may be personal, familial, or communal values. Others, however, may be values that you have recently adopted in becoming part of the medical profession. These professional values are not yet as strong as the other types of values, due to their recent adoption, but you identify with them and aspire to uphold them as part of the goals of the profession. Wanting to voice and act on those values may be more difficult, both in terms of recognizing how they apply to a given situation as well as how confident you might be in acting to uphold them, yet through practice and experience in choosing to uphold them, it will get easier to identify with them and demonstrate your appreciation of them in practice.

Second, medical students have voiced their values at some point in the past, and these experiences can serve as a starting point for voicing their values as medical professionals. Medical ethics and professionalism is not a category unto itself, wholly distinct from the moral choices people make in their everyday lives. There are many instances where you have acted on your values and created habits that are easily translatable to ethical and professional behavior in the medical context as well. A simple example, which is not an ethical challenge per se but can still clarify the idea that a person can rely on personal experience to help their professional training, would be in learning how to maintain good eye contact as a sign of respect while taking patient histories. When taking a patient history, medical students must at the same time think about the next question to ask, how a patient's history impacts his or her differential diagnosis, what physical examination maneuvers to perform, and take notes. All of this demands a large cognitive load for students, making it challenging for them to remember to demonstrate respect and maintain eye contact. However, there are other times outside of the medical context when you are busy but also want to uphold the value of respecting others. For example, when at a checkout counter, you must unpack groceries from your cart, grab money or a credit card, bag the groceries, etc., but if you practice maintaining eye contact with the checkout person and other people in your everyday life, you may be able to use that experience as a way to make it easier to try to keep eye contact with your patients as well, since it becomes natural for you to do so. So too in cases where you might face ethical and professional challenges, you should look to experiences upon which you can rely as examples to act in similar ways.

Third, the more one can practice voicing his or her values, the more one can improve in responding to frequently encountered conflicts. Ethics, when put into action, entails skills like many other practical fields, in that practice and repetition will lead to improvement. Practice will lead to improvement in the efficacy of your attempts as well as in increasing the amount of effort you can withstand before becoming too tired or frustrated, thereby becoming unable to be effective. By practicing how to voice and act on your values through creating scripts and simulating how you might act in an ethical challenge, you can improve your skills and gain habits in an environment where the stakes might be lower than in real life. This would be similar to going over plays and scrimmaging weeks before your first game. The practice allows a person to develop and become more comfortable playing "when it counts." Practicing scripts in front of teachers and other students also provides opportunities for others to cooperatively and constructively offer suggestions that might improve your own strategies and scripts. It also allows all students to learn from each other to come up collaboratively with tools that each can adopt based on each individual's own personal strengths and weaknesses. It also sets up an environment where students learn that they can depend on each other for ethical and practical guidance when they might be faced with a challenge.

Fourth, it is easier for a person to voice his or her values in some contexts than others. Because ethics entails skills, it is not the case that one is either ethical or not. Rather, there will be times where the ethical option is much harder to choose or to act upon than other times. Being faced with a situation where acting on your values is difficult should not be a reason to despair or to give up on your professional identity. Sometimes the difficulty might stem from your own vulnerabilities or limitations; other times the organizational structure might preclude you from being able to act on your values. Knowing if it is the former or the latter might also help you to understand what avenues there might be to improve or make it easier to voice your values in the future.

Fifth, each student's example is powerful and can empower others. No one needs to see himself or herself as being alone. We shouldn't assume that we are the only ones who have values and want to act on them. Most of the time, people have different views over what is occurring, have different goals for what they want to achieve, or have different ways of prioritizing values. Especially in an interprofessional context, members of different professions may disagree as to what the health care team could and should do because of the different scopes of practice or goals each profession brings with it. Rather than thinking that you might be the only person who wants to do the right thing, it would be more accurate and productive to think that you are not alone. Your colleagues also want to act on their own values and, collaboratively, the team wants to act on the values that they share in ways that reinforce everyone's ethical integrity. Therefore, if one person is empowered to give voice to his or her values, it may lead to a positive domino effect, where others will also join the effort. Moreover, you may not know who you might empower through your own actions. You may find allies in places you never expected. You should be open to helping others help you, whomever they might be.

Sixth, the better a person knows himself or herself, the more he or she can prepare to play to his or her strengths and, when necessary, protect himself or herself from weaknesses. Self-knowledge is important both for decision-making and for acting. In terms of decision-making, we are all affected by certain unconscious biases which will lead us to reasoning towards a certain position which we would not support if we were aware of how our biases were influencing us. Also, knowing whether it is easier for you to find allies or speak alone will help you determine which route would be best for you to pursue in acting on your values. We will discuss self-knowledge to a greater extent in later sections, when we go into further detail about how self-knowledge affects the way we approach ethical decision-making and how we carry out the moral choices we make.

Seven, the more a person believes it's possible to voice and act on his or her values, the more likely he or she will be to do so. In his essay, *The Sentiment of Rationality*, William James gives the following anecdote: Suppose yourself to be like a mountain climber who has found himself in a position whereby he has to jump across a bit of a chasm. Never being in such a position, the climber has no experience to know whether he will make the jump or not. He continues,

> but hope and confidence in myself make me sure I shall not miss my aim, and nerve my feet to execute what without those subjective emotions would perhaps have been impossible. But suppose that, on the contrary, the emotions of fear and mistrust preponderate; or suppose that, having just read the Ethics of Belief, I feel it would be sinful to act upon an assumption unverified by previous experience, – why, then I shall hesitate so long that at last, exhausted and trembling, and launching myself in a moment of despair, I miss my foothold and roll into the abyss.[25]

In many ethical challenges, we may feel like that climber who is stuck between a rock and a hard place, with a gaping hole we must jump over or fall into. In cases like these, it is not beneficial or productive to complain about the situation we are in, or how we got here, or whose fault it is. It is also not helpful to think that we can do nothing about it, for then we will certainly fall into the abyss. But if we believe we can achieve what we need to do and we step confidently to do it, we will have a greater probability of success than otherwise.

This last assumption, while important in and of itself, can help speak to the previous ones as well. Students may not have these assumptions yet. They may need more experience to see why these assumptions are worth having. However, in learning how to give voice and act on their values, they should suspend disbelief and act as if they have them. Only if they rely on them, albeit even if just contingently at first, can the assumptions really serve as foundations for moral empowerment. If one does not accept them or suspects them, then the practice of giving voice to values will not serve its pedagogical goals.

Notes

1 Stern, D. T. (2006). *Measuring Medical Professionalism*. Oxford University Press, 18.

2 Buck, E., Holden, M., & Szauter, K. (2017). Changes in humanism during medical school: a synthesis of the evidence. *Medical Science Educator, 27*(4), 887–893.
Mostaghimi, A., Olszewski, A. E., Bell, S. K., Roberts, D. H., & Crotty, B. H. (2017). Erosion of digital professionalism during medical students' core clinical clerkships. *JMIR Medical Education, 3*(1).

3 *Measuring Medical Professionalism*, 5.

4 Hegazi, I., & Wilson, I. (2013). Medical education and moral segmentation in medical students. *Medical Education, 47*(10), 1022–1028.

5 This contradicts Kohlberg's theory of moral reasoning as a structured whole, as well as his premise that once a person attains a higher level of thinking he or she does not revert to a lower level later. To explain their findings, Hegazi and Wilson attributed the decline in moral judgment competence specifically for medical dilemmas to moral segmentation rather than inhibition. They also posited that moral segmentation is due to the influence of the hidden curriculum in hospital systems that negatively socialize medical students during their rotations. This assumption, however, does not explain how students decreased in moral judgment competence based on a Kohlbergian model, since it contradicts both the structured whole assumption as well as the assumption that people do not revert to previous stages of moral development.

6 Feitosa, H. N., Rego, S., Bataglia, P. U. R., Sancho, K. F. C. B., Rego, G., & Nunes, R. (2013). Moral judgment competence of medical students: a transcultural study. *Advances in Health Sciences Education, 18*(5), 1067–1085.

7 Slováčková, B., & Slováček, L. (2007). Moral judgement competence and moral attitudes of medical students. *Nursing Ethics, 14*(3), 320–328.

8 Haidt, J. (2001). The emotional dog and its rational tail: a social intuitionist approach to moral judgment. *Psychological Review, 108*(4), 814.

9 Haidt, J., & Joseph, C. (2004). Intuitive ethics: How innately prepared intuitions generate culturally variable virtues. *Daedalus, 133*(4), 55–66.

10 Another difference between the two approaches is that Kohlberg takes a prescriptive view of what moral development should entail, thereby imagining any influence that counters the intended moral growth to be a "hidden curriculum," while Haidt takes a descriptive view of what moral development does entail, thereby accepting the moral ethos of each environment to be taken without judgment.

11 Smith, C., Christoffersen, K., Davidson, H., & Herzog, P. S. (2011). *Lost in Transition: The Dark Side of Emerging Adulthood*. OUP, USA.

12 See footnote 10. Also, for more information on the relationship between prescribed trajectories for moral development and the influence of situational factors on that development, see Maimonides for Moderns, pp. 233–238, on the relationship between situationism and dispositionism.

13 www.abms.org/media/84742/abms-definition-of-medical-professionalism.pdf

14 http://abimfoundation.org/what-we-do/physician-charter

15 Cohen, J. B., Myckatyn, T. M., & Brandt, K. (2017). The importance of patient satisfaction: A blessing, a curse, or simply irrelevant?. *Plastic and Reconstructive Surgery, 139*(1), 257–261. Paddison, C. A., Abel, G. A., Roland, M. O., Elliott, M. N., Lyratzopoulos, G., & Campbell, J. L. (2015). Drivers of overall satisfaction with primary care: evidence from the English General Practice Patient Survey. *Health Expectations, 18*(5), 1081–1092.

16 In the previous paragraph, I equated "professionalism" with virtues, while here it is equated with values. Values differ from virtues in that values are the priorities that a community imparts; virtues, on the other hand, are the capabilities that adherents develop so that those values can be adopted and expressed in behavior. As such, professionalism is a value when seen from the perspective of the *profession's priorities* and a virtue when seen from the perspective of the *professional's capacities*.
17 http://abimfoundation.org/what-we-do/physician-charter
18 Gaita, R., & Taylor, G. (1981). Integrity. *Proceedings of the Aristotelian Society*, Supplementary Volumes, *55*, 148.
19 McFall, L. (1987). Integrity. *Ethics, 98*(1), 5–20.
20 Cohen, J. J. (2006). "Professionalism in medical education, an American perspective: from evidence to accountability." *Medical Education, 40*(7), 607–617.
21 Irwin, T. (2000). *Nicomachean Ethics*. Hackett Publishing, 3.
22 Attribution theory is a social psychology theory that suggests that people act as naïve psychologists and try to infer why people do certain things. The reason to make such inferences is to understand other people's behavior and determine how to respond. Why people do things is seen as either dispositional or situational, and one's response and feelings toward the person or behavior will be very different, given those two categorizations.
23 In her article, "Giving Voice to Values: A Pedagogy for Behavioral Ethics," Mary Gentile writes of this frame shift, "I have found that if one asks 'What would *you* do?' a sort of preemptive rationalization process is activated. Before a student even begins to consider how they might act ethically, they experience the countervailing arguments: maybe I do not have all the information; maybe it is not really wrong; maybe it is wrong, but it is not my responsibility; maybe it is wrong, but it is not possible to change the situation and I may even make things worse; and so on. Now of course, many of these arguments may be true or frequently true. But the impact of asking 'What would *you* do?' activates them, often preventing a creative and open exploration of whether there may actually be an effective strategy for acting ethically. This unconscious process of preemptive rationalization frees the student from the discomfort of a sort of cognitive dissonance that would come along with knowing something was wrong but doing it anyway. It is self-protective and entirely understandable. So, rather than exhorting students to simply override a natural tendency, GVV asks them to engage in the thought experiment. GVV never asks them to consider what they would do until after they have spent time thinking about how the protagonist could be effective, thereby enabling them to experience themselves as actually having a true and viable choice, rather than being required to martyr themselves to an ethical position." See Gentile, M. C. (2017). Giving Voice to Values: A pedagogy for behavioral ethics. *Journal of Management Education, 41*(4), 469–479.
24 Gentile, M. C. (2010). *Giving Voice to Values: How to Speak Your Mind When You Know What's Right*. Yale University Press, xxiii.
25 James, W. (1908). *The Will to Believe, and Other Essays in Popular Philosophy*. Longman's, Green, and Co., 7.

2

MAKING MORAL DECISIONS

Even though moral decision-making and moral action are two sides of the same lens and one should look through each side of that lens to arrive at a proper and efficacious action plan that gives voice to one's values, the two components – i.e. making a moral decision and acting on that decision – consist of different skills and face different challenges. Therefore, we will look at each side independently, both in terms of explaining those necessary skills and the challenges one faces, in the next two chapters. You will also practice developing those skills somewhat independently when engaged as small groups working on the first set of cases at the end of the book. For the last set of cases, you will finally bring the two sides of the moral lens together and practice how to make moral decisions that give voice to your values as well as how to act on them.

This chapter will provide a background into moral decision-making in general and how to apply moral decision-making to medical ethics education. It will explain the various steps of which moral decision-making consists. This includes recognizing one's own (and others') biases that influence what one sees as salient to the moral question at hand, identifying the relevant medical, social, and legal facts that inform the boundaries of what is deemed the set of proper decisions, and considering the overarching values and goals of the patient–physician relationship which help weigh those various options. The chapter will also provide an overview of the main ethical frameworks that medical ethicists use to reach their decisions. In doing so, I hope that this section will equip you with the basic knowledge of medical ethics so that you can develop skills to reach decisions by which you act on your values and build a positive identification with doing so. You may want to consult other, more theoretical, works to gain a deeper appreciation of ethical theories in medical ethics, and you will have to acquaint yourselves with medical law, hospital policies, and professional position papers when considering how to act in particular situations. However, this section allows for a good introduction into medical ethics and ethical decision-making so that you know how to approach challenges in the future. Additional concepts and particular professional values will also be further discussed at the end of each case to help guide you towards formulating proper ethical action strategies.

Many moral choices (and the choices we make more generally) are often intuitive, based on simple heuristics, or shaped by the environment in which we find ourselves. For example, the choice to give money to a homeless person on the street, not to sample produce at a farmer's market without paying for it, or to speak up when someone is being bullied is usually done without much forethought or deliberation. Rather, one acts (or not) based on simple rules of conduct, out of habit, depending on circumstances (whether we had a good night's rest, are with supportive friends, or are primed to act), or based on all of these factors to one degree or another. We are able to make such quick decisions in these types of cases because they are familiar to us. We can relate them to an experience where we had to make a similar choice in the past.

Consistency in the choices that we make allows us to adhere to, and to identify with, certain values that we hold dear. Moreover, these values, such as "help out another person when we can" or "don't take anything without paying for it," are easily comprehensible and have corresponding actions which they promote, making their adherence and our identification with them easily reinforceable. Whether these values were instilled in us as children or we adopted them later in life makes little difference, since, through acting on them we have made them our own. Choices based on these values seem almost to come from our gut, and we, at times, are unable even to express why these choices are the correct ones.

When we act according to consistent routines or when we are in an environment that encourages us to act our values, it is easy to do so. However, when everyone else is acting in ways that contradict our values, it becomes much more difficult to go against the tide. It is not impossible, but doing so requires either knowing how to put our own values into practice or an intellectual confirmation that those values are important in order to affirm that we want to act upon them. Oftentimes, we need both. In a challenging environment such as this, it is more difficult to rely simply on our gut reactions, since they may seem to be unachievable, either because we feel we cannot act alone or because we do not want to. In time, without learning how to reinforce our identification with our values and the importance we ascribe to acting on them, we may get swept up by the tide and lose those values to which we cannot give voice. Our gut reactions may begin to give way to gut rationalizations that justify why we should maintain the status quo rather than trying to change it.

It is also difficult to act on our values in situations that are new and different from our previous experiences. In cases like these, the difficulty does not necessarily stem from an oppositional culture. Rather, it stems from a difficulty in knowing how our values should be put into action given unfamiliar circumstances, or whether there are other values that we should consider that we have not previously had to. The difficulties we might encounter when making moral choices and acting on them in unfamiliar environments present a different type of challenge than when the environment is familiar but the people around us are acting in ways contrary to our values. In unfamiliar situations, the difficulty stems, not from our own internal conflict, but from our inexperience in knowing how to act on our values, both in terms of which values to adopt and what would be necessary for our choices to be achievable.

As a member of the medical profession, you will face many situations where a moral choice must be made. Some of those choices will be easy; the circumstances will be similar enough to non-professional experiences so that you will be able to make quick moral decisions. For example, choosing to uphold the value of patient confidentiality is similar enough to choosing to uphold the value of keeping a friend's secret. Similarly, speaking with other members of the collaborative care team about patients in a respectful manner is similar to the experience of speaking with any other group of teammates, friends, or acquaintances. This is not to say that they are exactly the same, but they are analogous enough for you to rely on non-professional experiences to think about how to act in professional circumstances.

Some choices, however, will be of the type where giving voice to your own values will go against the tide, and some choices – especially those in the beginning of your professional identity formation – will be of the type where you must consider new professional values when making the right choice or where you will find yourself in an unfamiliar environment, such as the organizational structure of the hospital or healthcare system in which you will work. Deciding what choice to make in these circumstances will entail much more deliberation and understanding of the environment in order to act successfully.

In healthcare settings, the complexity of deciding how to act on your values, where moral choices are laden with medical and social consequences for you, your healthcare team, and the patient for whom you are caring, demands that you not only consider your own values, but also how those values relate to others who will be affected by your decision, with primacy going to the patient. This means that as much as you want to act on your values, the choices that you make must take the potential consequences for the patient as primary. This does not mean that you must defer to the patient even against your own values, but it does mean that any alternative that you consider must incorporate ways for both your and the patient's values to be voiced and respected. Also, in addition to considering the different people who will be affected by your decision, you must also take into account medical law, professional standards, hospital policies and resources, on one side, and the abilities and motivations of patients and your colleagues to agree with and act on any decision you want to make, on the other side.

In sum, the factors that you need to consider in deciding how to act on your values include the medical knowledge inherent in the ethical question, the legal requirements and proscriptions that affect which decisions can be achievable, the organizational policies and culture which creates norms and general procedures that people follow, and the various stakeholders that will be affected by your decision, such as your patient and the members of the collaborative care team, whose values, roles, and priorities may be different from your own. This is in addition to your own personal and professional values to which you want to give voice and the personal strengths and weaknesses you have to confront in carrying out your decision. As such, any successful strategy must be deliberate, effortful, and orderly, in terms of the process of making a decision upon which to act and considering how your decision can be implemented efficaciously.

As you gain more experience, familiarity with your professional environment will make it easier to act on your values successfully. Yet this is only true if you learn and practice how to voice your values and create the habits to do so. This moral and professional training is not simply reactionary, though it should include reflection on how you have acted in the past in order to learn how to act more efficaciously in the future. In addition, the moral and professional training you will go through as part of any course that incorporates this book and the GVV methodology that it encompasses will consist of proactive exercises where you will imagine what decision you will make and how you could act on it to voice to your values successfully. Proactive training is not simply a means to practice in a low-stakes environment; it is an essential component, since it familiarizes you to think about how you could act in the future. It trains you not only to think about what choices you would want to make, but also in how to create a strategy to act on those choices. In going through the various hypothetical cases found in the latter part of the book – yet imagining that you are actually faced with those choices – you learn to appreciate and utilize the tools you already have at your disposal, what you need to make the best choice, and the legal and organizational factors that might either help or hinder you in acting on your decisions. You also learn to anticipate how other stakeholders might respond to your decisions and what consequences you might expect from your choices.

This chapter will go through the various components that factor into making moral decisions. It will explain why each component has been included, why it is relevant to the moral decision-making process, and how each component should be used in the practice of proactively making moral decisions. You should use this chapter as an introduction to ethical decision-making, as well as review it when, for the first set of cases, you will have to discuss the ethical reasons behind the decisions the protagonists make, and, for the second set of cases, when having to make decisions for yourself. At the beginning, when engaged in cases, you may find yourself spending lots of time on one or another aspect of moral decision-making, or getting sidetracked in a way that does not move you towards the goal of coming to an ethical decision. When that happens, you should try to be disciplined and work through the decision-making process, even if you feel that you have not fully explored all of the ramifications of the particular aspect of the process. Similarly, if you feel that you do not have enough time or knowledge to consider what each step of the process asks of you, try to complete each step to the best of your ability. Oftentimes, you must make the best ethical decision you can, given your limitations, both in terms of your knowledge and experience as well as of time. Choosing not to make a decision because of your perceived limitations is making a choice not to act. As you practice thinking about why a protagonist's decision is morally justified and deliberating on your own decisions, you will find that you will become better at staying on the task of being action-oriented. You will also find that you will become better and quicker at going through the various steps.

While it might look like these steps, i.e. recognizing your and others' biases, identifying salient facts and values, and applying different ethical frameworks to reach a conclusion, occur in a linear fashion, you should apply the different steps recursively, so that any step allows you to check your previous steps as well as prepare you for the next one. In this way, the different steps in moral decision-making help you improve your skills as well as keep you mindful of the true goal, i.e. reaching a conclusion that is based on your values. For example, examining which biases might be affecting your gut reaction allows you to see your gut reaction for what it is, and it also allows you to be more open to perceiving and recognizing the salient facts and values that the case includes. While recognizing and prioritizing facts and values you not only identify what is pertinent to the case, but you also become aware of how your biases might have caused you to miss something as well as become prepared to make the decision that you want to make. By considering your decision in light of the different ethical frameworks, you will be able to see how your decision prioritizes different facts and values, and whether it does so in the ways that you really want.

The gut reaction

As discussed earlier, moral decision-making in healthcare situations often incorporates deliberate, effortful, and orderly thinking – what Daniel Kahneman's calls "System 2 processes." According to Kahneman, decision-making consists of two types of processes, "System 1" and "System 2." These are not actually two separate agents within a person's mind, yet their distinction allows Kahneman to describe these processes, so that we can focus on how the systems operate in coming to conclusions rather than how they work biologically. System 1 processes generate gut reactions; they are automatic and occur quickly, whereby a person is not aware or does not feel in control of the process.[1] System 2 processes, on the other hand, are effortful and require attention and concentration. The systems often work in tandem, where System 1 identifies familiar situations, recognizes simple patterns, and provides immediate initial reactions; while System 2 serves as a check on System 1 when patterns or reactions demand more complex analysis and moderating (such as in many medical professional situations). However, because System 2 processes require more energy, activation of System 2 processes are intentional, meaning that one runs the risk of relying simply on System 1 if one is not careful or under a high cognitive load.

Without developing your System 2 processes so that they can be activated and effective in high-stress environments, it will be difficult to engage in moral decision-making and create action strategies when these situations occur. Yet, as you develop your skills through practice, it will become easier to rely on them, even in unfamiliar or stressful environments. For example, think about doing calculus while driving in traffic. It may be difficult to calculate an integration or differential while driving. However, consider a mathematician who is driving in traffic. Because he or she has spent more time devoted to practicing calculus, it will be easier for him or her than for you. While the calculus example applies to quantitative thinking, it is the same idea for many different types of performances. When one joins a sports team, players endlessly do drills to build their particular skills in practice, then they scrimmage to see how those particular skills form skillful plays, and only then do they start their season, playing under the stress of the live game. Similarly, actors rehearse lines, then scenes, then have dress rehearsals, and only then do they open the show for a live audience.

In the same way, through the practice of creating strategies and scripts that implement your moral choices, not only can you rely on those strategies and scripts in similar situations in the future, but you will also build skills to apply in new situations, thereby reducing your cognitive load when you need to rely on those skills in the future. As your skills improve, some of the components that were originally part of System 2 will become part of System 1 processes. Practice and creating habits which make certain decisions less effortful is a foundation in virtue ethics, which holds as a premise that one's values (as shaped by one's habits) are intimately tied to one's ability for practical reasoning.

Without practice, however, your System 2 processes will come to reinforce your System 1 conclusions by providing justifications or rationalizations for your immediate responses, as opposed to offering further analysis. This is because when people have gut reactions, they usually don't investigate what might be influencing their judgments. When they do provide reasons for their gut reactions, they often justify why their reaction is correct rather than explaining the reasons for that reaction. When this occurs, the System 2 processes work to provide rationalizations for the chosen answer and do not deliberate as to whether that answer is correct or not. Yet, through practice, you will become better at integrating your System 1 and System 2 processes so that you can proactively act based on reasons for acting rather than reactively justifying your actions by offering rationalizations.

This does not mean that gut reactions are never thoughtful, only that the person is not aware of the thought process which is occurring. Remember, gut reactions rely on the thinking tools, such as heuristics, that have already become natural and familiar, so that we do not have to begin from first premises whenever we have to make mundane choices in our daily lives. The difficulty of relying on gut reactions in complicated situations is that there is usually not a simple answer to complicated questions. Alternatively, what may seem to be analogous to a simple situation may in fact not be. We may therefore be relying on the wrong tools, which will cause us to act against what we really want to do. As you make your gut reactions more explicit, analyze what might be influencing those reactions, and practice approaching ethical questions from the view of acting on your own values, you will eventually be able to "re-wire" your instinctive responses to be make values-driven action more likely.

Therefore, when developing your skills of ethical decision-making and acting, be as deliberate in your ethical thinking as you are in your clinical and diagnostic thinking. However, because moral choices are much more personal than the diagnoses we try to discover, it becomes much more difficult to determine quickly whether our moral, as opposed to our diagnostic, choices are the best ones or not. Therefore, we won't recognize whether we are thinking fast and rationalizing our quickly-made choices, or actually reasoning toward the best answer, unless we recognize the different thought-processing systems and the distinctions between the two. As such, even for "simple" cases, where our gut reactions may end up to be correct, it is important to slow down and analyze our decisions to see if they truly are in line with our values first, and then think about how we could enact them. In fact, it is often easier to work with "simple" cases in the beginning so that we can focus on developing skills rather than getting the best answers. Think of it as doing drills and practicing lines, which are meant to hone our skills to act quicker and with more ease, so that it will be more natural to do so during the live event, or, in our case, in more complicated situations.

When going through the medical ethics cases at the end of this book where you are asked to make a decision, even though your gut reactions may not end up being the best answer, it is still helpful to start with recognizing what they are. The purpose of starting with your immediate response, rather than starting with examining your understanding of the facts and values on a given situation, is that you are usually unaware of how your fast thinking is shaping your perception. Moreover, it is easier to examine or analyze something concrete than to imagine what might be affecting a person in the abstract. As such, starting with recognizing and then critiquing your gut reaction to uncover your unconscious processing is a way to force yourself to confront your fast thinking and to force you to slow down and analyze. This in turn, allows you to recognize how your understanding of the relevant facts and values of the case are influenced by your biases, which will allow you to consider openly how you can prioritize facts and values through ethical thinking

The point, therefore, is not always to be right in your gut reactions, and the gut reaction is not meant to measure how good you are in conceiving the best choice. After deliberation, you might not end up aligning with your original idea. However, even if you determine that your gut reaction is the best choice, there is a big difference between going with your gut and making a reasoned decision, even if the answer is the same. The difference lies in the process and defensibility of your choices. In other words, how you get to an answer is as important as the answer itself, especially since we want to prepare ourselves for making choices in the future. Lucky guessing is not a tool for good moral or clinical thinking.

One way to look at this idea is through comparison with the definition of knowledge in the field of epistemology, where knowledge is defined as "justified true belief." When a belief is true but not justified (such as in a gut reaction), you might end up with the right answer but still not know the concept or idea properly. It might just be a lucky guess. We can think of justifiability using the "AAA" model of evaluation developed by Ernest Sosa:

1. A belief is *accurate* if and only if it is true.
2. A belief is *adroit* if and only if it is produced skillfully.
3. A belief is *apt* if and only if its determination as true comes from the believer's skill in assessing its truth-value (as opposed to luck).

While this may apply to knowledge of facts, it can also apply to moral decision-making. A moral choice is *accurate* if it is based on one's values; it is *adroit* if it is arrived at through skilled moral decision-making; and it is *apt* if the person identifies with the decision based on his or her own reasoning. The "AAA" model of evaluating moral decision-making allows us to reflect on the choices that we make, how we make them, and our ability to see them as our own.

These concepts are important in trying to understand our gut reactions, and why it is critical that you identify your gut reaction first. When critiquing your gut reaction to uncover the biases you may have, you might imagine other ways to describe or respond to the situation. This is a productive exercise to recognize when you might be influenced by your biases. It will also help to cultivate empathy. Yet seeing other ways to respond to a situation is not the same as taking a devil's advocate position. Looking at other ways to respond to a situation is a way to check your own biases. It allows you to gather all the facts and values that pertain to a situation so that you can reason to an answer. Taking a devil's advocate position creates a situation where a person is looking at different conclusions and then seeing with which conclusion they feel more comfortable. It inclines you towards starting with a conclusion and working to justify it rather than starting with facts and values and reasoning to the best conclusion.

Moral awareness: bias check

After you have identified your gut reaction, you will start to consider why you had that reaction. People are often unaware of their biases or the impact their biases may have on their attitudes or their decision-making; therefore, making yourself aware of your biases will help to ensure that your choices and actions are in line with the values you want to voice. We will not go through all the potential biases here; rather, we will go through three which have the greatest effect on moral perception in group and healthcare settings, namely, the conformity bias, obedience to authority, and the framing bias. Conformity bias and obedience to authority are particularly important, since healthcare is very hierarchical yet also collaborative, and it is sometimes a challenge to know when we are letting the tide take us versus when we must be open to learning from others' perspectives. Similarly, in recognizing the framing bias we become aware of how we and others limit possible good choices when we refuse to see situations through various different perspectives.

Conformity bias

Conformity bias is the tendency people have to behave or think like those around them rather than using their own personal judgment. From a perspective of moral growth, conformity often allows those who are newly initiated into a profession to adopt practices and habits that might be foreign or uncomfortable when part of normal, everyday life (such as performing a physical exam), but when seen through the lens of professional practice they are valuable competencies that the profession demands. In such cases, suspending one's personal judgment to allow oneself to be open to learning is important. Sometimes, however, conformity bias is an obstacle to develop good moral and professional habits. Even if there are certain habits or behaviors that are uniquely appropriate to given professions, most of the time patient–physician encounters or inter-professional encounters entail the same social norms that are part of everyday interactions. When professionals improperly rely on an unethical culture to justify bad behavior, conformity bias will usually reinforce bad habits rather than let people learn good ones. Moreover, if a given habit or behavior is uniquely appropriate, there should be good reasons to explain how it developed and why it is important, so that a person can use his or her own personal judgment to identify with it, rather than justify it because everyone else acts the same way.

Conformity bias not only affects whether one might act on one's values or not, it also affects how one perceives relevant facts and values. An example where conformity bias affects one's ability even to perceive a simple fact is seen through the Asch experiments. In the 1950s, Solomon Asch conducted an experiment where he asked a group of people to say which of four lines was the longest. Only one person in the group was an actual subject of the experiment; all others in the group were part of the experiment. One line was clearly longer than the others, yet all of the people in the group, except the subject, would say that a particular line was longer, even though it wasn't. Overall, 75% of actual subjects of the experiment gave at least one incorrect answer. One could say that the Asch experiment measured how people conformed their actions to the group and not how people's perception or thinking conformed to group consensus, since the subjects could have known the correct answer but conformed to the group anyway. However, the psychological literature notes that the Asch experiments demonstrate that, in fact, subjects questioned their own perceptions and changed their belief in what they saw rather than simply lying to the experimenter by claiming that the wrong line was the longest. The Asch experiment demonstrates that the conformity bias is largely unconscious, and that the pressure to conform affects even one's thoughts and beliefs. It is, therefore, important to be aware and actively reflect on whether one might be influenced by this bias when making moral decisions.

In her book, *From Detached Concern to Empathy*, Dr. Jodi Halpern provides a medical example of how the conformity bias can affect clinical decisions. She tells of her experience as a trainee in psychiatry when she was working with a 56-year-old woman with diabetes mellitus who just had her second above-the-knee amputation. The woman had a long history of kidney failure and required dialysis three days a week, but, after the surgery, she refused to continue dialysis and would not tell the medical team why she made her decision. The team called for a psychiatric consultation to gauge her capacity to make her decision. When Dr. Halpern asked her if anything else was hurting her besides her body, the woman reluctantly said that her husband had told her that he no longer loves her and that he wanted to be with someone else, since he could no longer be attracted to her after losing both her legs.

Dr. Halpern told the medical team about the woman's abandonment by her husband. The physicians on the medical team responded by saying that they understood that her predicament was sorrowful, yet, she reports, they said, "But think about it humanely. What kind of life does she face now? Wouldn't you want to die if you had lost your spouse, your legs, your kidneys, and faced future blindness and other medical problems? Let's not ask her any more questions, let's just make her as comfortable as possible and accept her decision to die."[2] The medical team continued to focus on the patient's right to die, even though Dr. Halpern felt personally conflicted about the social – rather than simply medical – factors that influenced that decision. In the end, the medical team deemed that the woman was competent to refuse treatment and she died soon thereafter.

Regardless of the many ethical questions about how to determine capacity and the right to refuse treatment that this case engenders, the medical team's conformity bias – in that they continued to conceive of the patient as a competent person who wanted to exercise her right to refuse treatment despite their discomfort with the underlying personal factors that led to her decision – prevented them from giving any serious consideration to what, if any, other alternatives they could have taken. Though they were sensitive to the woman's situation, the professional ethos of the medical team did not allow them to consider it as a factor in determining how to respond to her desire to refuse treatment. The medical team therefore either dismissed, or relegated as irrelevant, the patient's situation because they were subjected to a conformity bias, which relied on common practice and norms without considering the reasons for those norms and how they should be applied in a situation where a woman had quickly changed her perceptions due to the emotional and physical trauma she recently endured. This limited their decision-making to focusing on her eloquence in verbalizing her desire at the expense of considering if they could ameliorate the emotional and situational factors that influenced that desire.

Dr. Halpern was unable to act successfully to voice her objection in a way that could persuade the medical team. Yet, if before confronting the medical team, she asked herself, "What if you were going to act on your values – what would you say and do?" she may have been able to devise a strategy to anticipate the objections that the medical team had, or at least uncover the conformity bias that they held, especially since they did understand the predicament the patient was in. Alternatively, she could have helped the patient see what was influencing her decision to refuse treatment so that she might be open to other alternatives. Without asking how she might be able to act on her values, Dr. Halpern was caught in the position of following the medical team's position rather than trying to advocate for herself and her patient to discuss and implement any other strategy. This is not to say that one will always be successful when trying to give voice to one's own values, but it does allow a person a chance to be successful.

Obedience to authority

Obedience to authority is similar to the conformity bias, but the pressure comes from a superior in the given hierarchy rather than from one's colleagues. Again, just as there is a benefit for new initiates to mimic and defer to their superiors in order to learn, obedience to authority can also be a productive way for students to learn how to embody professional practice and the competencies that the profession demands. However, when authority figures act in ways that challenges one's personal moral sense, it may not be a lack of experience that makes a subordinate uncomfortable. The authority figure may be acting unethically. When that occurs, a subordinate must be able to consider whether what a superior is demanding is right rather than simply follow orders.

This type of bias occurs rather frequently, and the following examples demonstrate how strong this bias can be. One famous historical example comes from the defense of Nazi physicians at the Nuremberg War Criminal Trials. At the trials, the physicians' defense, called the "Nuremberg defense," for committing human atrocities was that they were just following orders from their superiors. This defense was not accepted by the judges of the trial.

Yet the obedience to authority bias does not only affect those who we consider evil perpetrators of atrocities. The effect of the bias on everyday people was researched through the experiments done by Stanley Milgram in the 1960s. In fact, Milgram was originally motivated to conduct his experiments by the trial of Adolf Eichmann, who argued that he was "just following orders" as a defense for his involvement in sending Jews to the Nazi death camps. In Milgram's experiments, a person is asked to test another person who is behind a wall and to give painful electric shocks to the person if he or she offers an incorrect answer. The subject believes that the person is actually receiving electric shocks, even though the subject in truth only hears pre-recorded sounds for each shock given. Before starting the test, the subject receives a shock so that he or she can feel what it would be like for the person being tested, yet during the experiment the subject is told that the voltage would increase in 15-volt increments for each wrong answer. After a number of wrong answers, the subject would hear the test-taker bang on the wall and complain about a heart condition, yet if the subject wanted to stop, he or she would be told either:

1. "Please continue,"
2. "The experiment requires that you continue,"
3. "It is absolutely essential that you continue," or
4. "You have no other choice, you *must* go on."

The results of the experiments showed that despite their discomfort 65% of people administered the experiment's final massive 450-volt shock. More recent, and less controversial, experiments have confirmed Milgram's findings, namely, that people's sense of responsibility is reduced whenever someone else orders a person to do something, regardless of whether the order is morally blameworthy or praiseworthy.[3] Other researchers, such as Jerry Burger, have identified four features that make obedience to authority more difficult to counteract, namely:

1. when the degree of change in an order increases incrementally,
2. if the situation in which obedience is demanded is novel or one where the person obeying is not familiar with the relevant information,
3. there is opportunity to deny or delegate responsibility, and
4. there is limited time or opportunity to think about one's decisions.[4]

Recognition of these additional considerations can allow a person who either is under pressure to obey an authority figure or who views a situation from an obedience bias to mitigate the situational factors that add to that pressure or bias so as to be able to overcome it.

An example from medical education occurs when a physician asks a medical student to do something and a student defers to the physician's authority, even if it may not be proper. Consider this once common example. A third-year medical student has just begun a clerkship in obstetrics and gynecology. She is considering OBGYN as a career choice, and she is excited that the rotation will allow her a lot of opportunity for hands-on learning. One day, she scrubs in for surgery on a patient who has benign fibroid tumors of the uterus. While the patient is under general anesthesia, the attending surgeon does a pelvic exam and explains to the students what he is doing. He then says that it is an ideal time for students to practice performing a pelvic exam because the patient will feel no discomfort or embarrassment. The students will also be able to learn much more on someone under general anesthesia than on an alert patient because the muscles are relaxed. After a few students have already examined the patient, the attending asks the particular student to go next. She hesitates, wondering whether the patient is undergoing too much or would even want so many students examining her while under anesthesia. Yet she nevertheless decides to perform the exam because she figures that the physician knows what he is doing. This student was right to be concerned since the students were not told whether the woman consented to these unnecessary exams. In fact, the Committee on Ethics of the American College of Obstetricians and Gynecologists reaffirmed its policy in 2017 that "pelvic examinations on an anesthetized woman that offer her no personal benefit and are performed solely for teaching purposes should be performed only with her specific informed consent obtained before her surgery."[5] Yet her rationalization that the physician knows what he is doing gave her a way to defer moral responsibility onto him rather than seeing the situation as an opportunity to voice her concerns.

Framing

Framing occurs when a person views a situation in a particular way which affects his or her understanding of the facts; the frame one chooses therefore influences how he or she determines right from wrong. For example, if someone views a hospital policy regarding end-of-life care in terms of the limited resources of a hospital, he or she may highlight different points than if he or she views it in terms of the autonomy of individual patients. Framing might also result in ethical fading, which occurs when highlighting a certain view causes values and facts that do not fit so well in that frame to be less salient.

One of the biggest framing issues in thinking about medical ethics challenges is in whether to consider health care delivery a public, or a private, good. When seen as a public good, health care delivery is about making sure that a group of people, whether that be the country as a whole or different communities in particular, achieve certain levels of good health. Health care decisions, when seen through this frame, would emphasize how public health organizations and government agencies work together with hospitals and health care systems to provide access to care and ensure that people have clean water, clean air, and healthy food so that everyone benefits. Similarly, when considering treatment and prevention options, health care systems will consider social and environmental factors that affect the health of individuals through methods of population health, which is an approach to health care that claims that where and how people live influence the types of illnesses to which they are vulnerable and the treatment strategies they can pursue successfully. When seen as a private good, health care delivery is about treating individuals based on their own personal histories, resources, and life goals. This view sees health care as a personal responsibility of individuals, who make choices in their lives and live based on those choices. Health care systems provide services to individuals when needed and requested; they do not limit the options available to people based on group consensus.

Recognizing the frame that health care is a public good or viewing medical questions through the frame that health care is a private good affects every aspect of medical ethics and the health care delivery debate, from legislative debates over who should pay for health care to physician aid-in-dying and whether medical marijuana should be considered legal or not. Both sides in these controversies have sound arguments, but any productive answer would have to incorporate the perspectives of the opposing views.

As briefly stated above, training yourself to counteract your own biases so as to be open to other perspectives is a way to develop the skills of empathy. Dr. Jodi Halpern, the psychiatrist mentioned earlier, describes empathy as a form of emotional reasoning and the means by which a person can imagine the distinct experiences of another person. Empathy differs both from sympathy and detached objectivity. Through sympathy, a physician sees herself as sharing the experience of the patient. She does not see how the patient experiences her circumstances but rather the physician feels that both she and the patient experience the circumstances together. Sympathy keeps the person focused on herself but includes the patient as a factor that influences her own emotional state. Detached objectivity, on the other hand, attempts to remove any emotional influence from the decision-making process. It thereby denies the relationship between affective and cognitive influences on moral reasoning. Both of these strategies dismiss the uniqueness of the patient's experience and minimizes the patient's position as a stakeholder in any decision. For Halpern, empathy consists of curiosity and decentering. Through curiosity, physicians become open to the patient's state of mind by imagining how the patient must be experiencing her situation. This does not mean that the physician puts herself in the patient's shoes, since doing so might risk bringing the physician's beliefs, values, and personality into the thought experiment. Rather, curiosity demands that the physician ask what life must be like from the patient's perspective. It is a means to understand why the patient is responding to her experience in the way that she is and not how the physician would respond if put in the same situation. Trying to understand what a circumstance is like for another person is what Halpern means by decentering; it is taking oneself out of the center of focus to allow oneself to perceive the experience of another. By recognizing one's own biases and accounting for them through trying to see different perspectives of a given situation, one can hone one's skills to become both more empathetic as well as more effective in acting on one's values given the views and values of the other stakeholders. This becomes a cycle of personal and professional development.

Recognizing and prioritizing facts and values

After you have assessed the biases that might have led you to your gut reaction, you can now be more open to perceive and consider the relevant medical and social facts, and the professional and other stakeholder values, that pertain to the ethical challenge with which you are faced in order to come up with an ethical decision that incorporates all the necessary components to consider. This decision should incorporate what is at stake for all parties and should be informed by the relevant medical law, hospital policies and professional position statements related to case. In the next chapter, when we discuss the skills and challenges that relate to creating post-decision action strategies and scripts (which is the primary innovation of the GVV model), we will also discuss identification of stakes and risks to all parties, but in a different way. In the decision-making stage, incorporating the stakes and risks of others is for the purpose of engaging in stakeholder analysis to determine whose interests should be taken into account and to what extent when reaching a decision. In the post-decision stage, identifying the stakes and risks of others is for the purpose of allowing you to identify potential levers and approaches which can make acting on your decision a successful endeavor. These approaches include re-framing the situation, minimizing the risks for those you want to influence, and so on.

Every situation you encounter where you have to make a moral, professional choice will entail particular medical facts, laws, organizational policies, and stakeholders that are relevant to the situation at hand. Therefore, particular facts and norms of which you might not be familiar have been included after each of the case presentations to help you begin to think about them in practice. However, there are two over-arching values that should be discussed here which permeate professional practice, namely, patient autonomy and physician authority. These values are tied to the nature of the patient–physician relationship as well as the goals of the medical profession.

The patient–physician relationship

The patient–physician relationship has two major aspects that influence how both the physician and the patient see their own roles and the roles of each other. The first aspect recognizes the inherent equality between the members of the relationship. Both the physician and the patient enter into the relationship voluntarily, and both deserve to maintain their own integrity and values.[6] The second aspect of the patient–physician relationship recognizes the inherent differences between the roles of the physician and the patient. Physicians, by virtue of their role as healers, their training, and their experience, serve as authorities on medical treatment. Patients, due to the vulnerabilities inherent in being sick, are dependent on physicians and other health care providers for their care. In general, a patient's dependence on a physician and a physician's authority, stem from a number of factors, such as

1. the patient lacks – and a physician possesses – requisite medical knowledge and competence to heal,
2. the patient's fears or emotional state due to illness may affect his or her ability to make decisions, while the physician is not as emotionally affected as the patient or a family member and can therefore be more objective in understanding the facts of a given situation,
3. the nature of the health care system in general leaves the patient largely excluded from the processes of his or her medical care, from understanding how different health care professionals and health systems work together in providing care to how payment is calculated and made for treatment.

This second aspect, which recognizes the differences between the physician and the patient, can create either a negative dynamic, where the differences serve as a means to empower the physician to control the relationship, or a positive dynamic, where physicians offer guidance and patients expect their physicians to have their interests in mind. This positive dynamic reflects what is known as the fiduciary nature of the patient–physician relationship.[7] A fiduciary relationship is one in which one party, in this case the patient, is in a vulnerable position and thus trusts the other person in the relationship, in this case the physician, always to act for his or her sole benefit. Ideally, the duty of the fiduciary, here the physician, entails the highest standard of care and an absence of any conflict of interest.

Because the relationship between patient and physician is a fiduciary one, decisions regarding medical treatment must be based on the patient's needs and his or her ability to follow the prescribed course of treatment. They cannot be based on the costs of medical procedures, the interests of scientific investigation or notions of societal justice, since such considerations are not relevant to the patient's individual best interest.

Patient autonomy

One of the prime considerations in the patient–physician relationship is patient autonomy, which has become a first among equals as a value in healthcare. The rise in priority of autonomy in medical ethics corresponds to the decline of the paternalistic tradition where the physician had sole decision-making authority. From a legal perspective, autonomy in the medical setting is a right to be free from the interference by others. However, from an ethical standpoint, autonomy also entails respecting and sometimes even facilitating others' abilities to act on their own values as well. In a fiduciary relationship, respecting other people's agency, or their ability (both intellectually and physically) to fulfill their goals, implies that the person has the information needed to make a decision and can think rationally so as to make it. This means that patient autonomy is not only a patient value, it is also a professional value and its fulfillment a professional duty, since physicians must help patients achieve autonomy by informing them of their medical conditions, the various treatment alternatives they can undergo, and the different consequences and ramifications of each treatment alternative, so that they can make informed decisions.

Physicians' professional goals

There are two general professional goals of medicine, (1) to improve a patient's physical condition and (2) to improve his or her quality of life. These two primary goals will sometimes be in conflict, such as in cases relating to end-of-life care, yet they are oftentimes complementary. For example, improving a patient's health will often lead to the patient having a higher quality of life. Conversely, tending to the psychological and social aspects of a person's life will have positive results on his or her health. Even though these primary goals speak about "a patient" in general, one should not think of patients as simply opportunities to fulfill one's professional goals. Your patients are not simply a means for you to practice your clinical skills and to improve your professional abilities; caring for particular patients is the goal in itself. The personal relationship between physician and patient is what creates the goals of medicine and is what gives them value. Keeping this in mind will influence how you approach professionalism and the people for whom you care.

Physician authority and professional integrity

Physician authority can manifest in one of two ways, which will affect the interaction between physician and patient. When acting in an authoritarian manner, a physician relies on his or her authority to control the relationship. When acting in an authoritative manner, a physician recognizes that his or her authority creates a fiduciary responsibility in which the physician must act in the patient's best interests and where the patient is the ultimate decider of his or her own course of treatment.

Authoritarian behavior takes advantage of the power that a role provides, and, in this case, power is the result of the dependence that a patient has on his or her physician. Physicians can be perceived as being in a situation of power due to their knowledge, judgment, and position in the health care system. Authoritarian physicians attempt to control their patients' behavior and treatment regimens based on what they think is best for the patient, according to either their own standard of what constitutes medical beneficence[8] or what they believe the patient would want. In both cases, however, the patient obeys the physician and does not participate in the decision-making process. Authoritarian behavior relies on the imbalances of the patient–physician relationship to coerce or pressure patients to agree to a physician's recommendations simply because he or she as the physician has made the recommendation. Authoritarian behavior is thus paternalistic in nature.[9] It diminishes the value of patient autonomy for the sake of treatment.

Authoritative guidance, on the other hand, recognizes the dependencies of patients but does not rely on them to coerce patients to accept a certain type of care. Rather, authoritative guidance affirms that, despite a patient's dependence on others for his or her care, he or she also has interests and motivations that will affect whether the patient will listen to the physician and follow the physician's prescriptions. As such, authoritative guidance demands that physicians demonstrate to their patients why their suggestions are sound so that patients voluntarily accept them. To do so, physicians not only need to show their own competence but they must also show they are accounting for their patients' experiences and needs. The efficacy of the physician's communication will be dependent on how legitimate the patient perceives a physician's suggestions and not on the patient's perceived consequences if he or she does not comply with the physician's orders. Authoritative guidance relies on a patient's trust in his or her physician's competence and in the perception that his or her physician understands and appreciates the patient's point of view. It thus allows for physicians to maintain professional authority while still respecting patient autonomy.

While the rise in patient autonomy has benefited medical professionalism by incorporating the patient's wishes in the decision-making process, when patients make decisions that physicians believe are not in their best interest and are based on misunderstanding or bad information, physicians can face a conflict of values between prioritizing patient autonomy or prioritizing beneficence. Both options have negative consequences, since by prioritizing autonomy, the patient may not get the care he or she needs, and in prioritizing beneficence, the patient's autonomy is being dismissed. Some physicians choose not to interfere with patients' decisions, even when the bases of those decisions may be incorrect. When physicians prioritize patient autonomy over beneficence, their justifications usually follow the notion that patients have the right to make bad decisions and that right trumps the physician's duty to treat them. This is not to say that patients' decisions should be unilaterally overridden; rather, physicians should be more active in facilitating patient autonomy (in the sense of increasing patients' understanding and therefore agency) to ensure that patients can make better decisions. Other physicians prioritize beneficence over autonomy, and will justify that prioritization by saying that patients would agree to the decision if only they could understand and account for all the information that the physician has. Yet this statement discounts the patient and does not consider the responsibility of the physician in helping the patient understand relevant information.

Patient-centered care requires physicians to rely on their authority and patients to express their autonomy, with physician non-interference in decision-making when appropriate. While physicians should never act contrary to patients' expressed wishes, remember that patient autonomy is not only freedom from external pressure or restraint but also includes empowering patients with the ability to make sound decisions. When patients are not able to make sound decisions due to irrational decision-making processes or incorrect beliefs, physicians have an obligation to provide patients a means to correct their thinking or act in their best interests. Keep in mind, though, that not all beliefs are strictly factual and that many beliefs have social or value components that must be respected. In this case, physicians must be careful not to allow their own biases to hinder patient autonomy.

One note on values

One way to make it easier to act on one's values, especially in a situation where values might conflict, is to think that values entail choices. If one has a value that he or she holds dear, then the person has a choice as to whether they want to uphold that value or not. Seeing values as entailing choices allows people to take control over their decisions of how to act rather than seeing value-based norms as being imposed upon them. For example, if I value confidentiality, then it is easier for me to uphold that value when I think, "I am not the type of person who breaks confidentiality; therefore, I will not disclose this information," than if I were to think, "I can't break confidentiality." The reason why it is easier to uphold one's values when perceived as choices is that it gives a person a sense of empowerment when choosing to uphold them, as well as a goal which a person is motivated to pursue.[10] This is especially the case in medical ethics and professionalism, where the values inherent in the profession are instrumental for fulfilling the goal of being a good physician.

Ethical frameworks

Even though the GVV methodology attempts to get students to imagine the decisions they would make if they were able to give voice to their own values, this chapter includes a section on different ethical frameworks that are used in medical ethics for a number of reasons. First, many medical ethicists and medical professionals who are faced with ethical issues use these frameworks to make decisions. Therefore, becoming familiar with these frameworks will allow you to recognize the kinds of thinking patterns that others use. Second, this section will enable you to discern which values, and how values, influence the kinds of decision alternatives you may reach. For example, deontological ethics emphasizes the values of intentionality and adherence to one's duty as priorities, while consequentialist ethics rates different alternatives according to how their respective consequences fare according to a given set of preferences. The framework by which you judge your values and alternatives will affect which options you might choose. Knowing the different frameworks can also mitigate getting stuck in a framing bias or being subject to ethical fading. We will see examples of this below. Third, you can use this section as a way to adopt tools and develop skills for your own decision-making. It may be the case that you reason to a choice that does not utilize any of the ethical frameworks discussed in this section; in fact, practical reasoning, which is a prime component in virtue ethics, purposefully does not see reasoning in formulaic terms like the ethical frameworks described below. Yet, by knowing how these frameworks arrive at ethical conclusions, it will be easier for you to critique your own judgments if you have alternative philosophical frames to which you can compare your own decision-making.

In traditional ethics and moral philosophy, there are two separate, but related, questions which are outside of the GVV "post-decision" methodology, but could be translated in such a way that reinforces the methodology. This first is – "*Is there a moral obligation that is independent of our own personal wants, desires, or beliefs?*" There are ethical theories that deny the existence of moral obligations outside of our own personal wants, desires, or beliefs.[11] Yet, for the most part, ethics and moral decision-making presumes that what one should do is not always what one wants to do, though it may be the case that a person always wants to do the right or good thing (which is a wonderful moral aspiration). What is important about this first question is that once you recognize that moral obligations are not simply based on your personal wants, desires, or beliefs, you will see that when you assert a moral judgment and try to persuade others to agree to enact the moral choice you want to make, you will realize that you will be more successful in persuading others when you provide a basis or explanation for why that judgment is convincing other than "that is what I think or want."[12] Even if your answer is "correct," when you simply assert what you want, your answer will not be justified or persuasive. This question should not detract from the main question of "How can I act on my values?" Instead, it should be seen as a way to begin to think of ways by which one may do so. In other words, you can translate the ethical question, "Is there a moral obligation that is independent of my own personal wants, desires, or beliefs?" to "How can I communicate my desire to act on my values in a way that speaks to shared conceptions and goals, instead of insisting that we do so simply because I want to?"

The second question, once ethicists presume that there is a moral obligation that one should try to fulfill, is – "*How can I fulfill that obligation in the best way possible?*"

The answer to this question includes not only what you choose to do and your intention to do so, but also the consequences that may result and how the choices you make help shape your identity. It also includes the manner in which you carry out that choice, in terms of the efficacy of the strategies you use and your ability to see the choice through. The first part of the answer speaks primarily to the decision-making process, while the second part of the answer speaks primarily to the ability for moral action. Remember, however, that these two parts are not wholly distinct, but rather they are integrated so that each aspect informs the other.

Each of the three major ethical frameworks or approaches that are used to think about how to make moral decisions has a different way to answer this second question, "*How can I fulfill that obligation in the best way possible?*" These frameworks are important to understand because they impact the way medical ethicists make decisions. They are:

1. Deontology (Kantianism) or a duty-based approach,
2. Consequentialism (utilitarianism) or an ends-based approach, and
3. Principlism or a principle-based approach.

While each ethical framework claims to be a comprehensive approach to ethical decision-making, it is best to see them as complementing each other. In everyday practical decision-making, ideas such as "good" and "right" are hard to define in simple terms and it is usually better to see how they interact with other concepts as well as the practical details of a given situation than to try to define them abstractly and then apply them formulaically. Also, each of these frameworks make certain assumptions about how to define and utilize concepts such as "good" and "right," as well as different ways to achieve them. In general, however, it is proper to think of "good" as referring to the consequences of a decision and "right" as the appropriateness of the decision itself. Thinking about the concepts in this way shows that they measure different things. For example, the right choice may not lead to good outcomes, unless you define the appropriateness of a choice by the goodness of its consequences. Therefore, we need to understand how each framework would approach a given issue, how each framework prioritizes social facts and moral values, and then consider how the different frameworks could be used together to come up with the most ethical solution.

Deontological (Kantian) ethics

Deontological ethics starts with the idea that moral obligations exist as part of the fabric of the world and they are recognized through reason. Immanuel Kant, who is the founder of this moral philosophy, explains how one recognizes the existence of the moral law by first distinguishing between different types of imperatives which obligate people to act. The first type of imperative is one that is contingent on a goal that a person has. For example, if I want to be an ethics professor, then I ought to come to work on time, I ought to deliver the content of my courses clearly, and I ought to make sure that the students are given all of the materials for my courses in a timely manner. These "oughts" or imperatives, however, are only "oughts" for me if I want to be an ethics professor. Yet there is not an imperative that says I have to be an ethics professor. These imperatives; therefore, says Kant, cannot be moral imperatives (though they are not immoral either) since they are not independent of my own personal wants or desires. In a word, they are not based on pure or objective reason.

For Kant, a moral obligation has to be categorical, meaning that it must be absolute and not contingent on any goal that a person might have. This means that deontological ethics focuses on "right and wrong" independently from "good and bad," since any consideration to what one wants to achieve makes the choice dependent on a goal. Even acting according to what is deemed proper in pursuit of one's own sense of good or self-fulfillment would not be considered a moral imperative, since it is based on the goal of increasing happiness in the world or achieving self-fulfillment. Also, to be categorical, the imperative may not by qualified by exceptions; everyone must be obligated to fulfill the moral norm. In other words, given a situation the moral imperative would be the one that everyone should do in a similar circumstance. This is similar to the religious maxim – do unto others what you would want done unto yourself – as well as the principle of (procedural) justice – treat like cases alike. Only Kant and other deontologists give the imperative a more abstract and philosophical ring to it. In fact, they have two main ways of expressing the moral imperative:

1. Act in such a way that your actions represent what you would deem a universal law, and
2. Act in such a way that you treat humanity, never merely as a means to an end, but always at the same time as an end.

Kant's latter statement could be restated as, "Do not use people to further your own goals, but rather respect people for their own sake."

While the moral law applies to everyone equally, without exception and without privilege, what a person should do in applying the universal moral law in practice is predicated on the abilities he or she has. For example, if a person cannot swim, he or she does not have the moral obligation to dive into a lake to save someone from drowning. The person does have an obligation to try to save the person, but only in a way that could be successful. Instead of risking drowning oneself, the moral obligation to save the person in the lake might be to call for help. Similarly, if I were a first year medical student faced with a situation where all of a sudden the person next to me grabs his chest, claims he has shortness of breath, and then vomits, I wouldn't be obligated to act as a trained physician, but I would be morally obligated to act according to my abilities. This means that medical professionals, given their expertise, would have a more demanding duty to treat people than others would. Also, because medical professionals uphold certain professional norms and values that are not common to the general populace, those norms and values create additional duties to which medical professionals must adhere. For example, even though Kantian ethics upholds the notion that there is a universal duty not to lie, physicians must also uphold their professional duty to maintain confidentiality. In a situation where the two might be in conflict, a physician should not lie, but also should not break confidentiality; therefore, he or she should find a third way to handle that situation.

The second criterion in fulfilling one's moral obligation is related to one's motivation for fulfilling one's duty. Once one determines what one can and ought to do, the reason why someone acts, in this framework, will determine whether the action has moral value or not. In other words, a person can act in a way that is in line with his or her moral duty but not act morally in a deontological perspective. If one acts because it fulfills his or her personal goals, then even if the action is in line with the moral law, the person's intention precludes him or her from calling his or her actions moral. In this framework, an individual's intention is of primary importance to determine the moral value of his or her actions. Moreover, because, in a deontological frame, making the right choice is of primary moral importance, a person would not be held morally responsible for things that are outside of his or her control. For instance, taking the example earlier of the person with chest pain, if, given the medical student's knowledge and ability, the student's moral obligation would be to call the emergency services, and the medical student calls, yet not with the intention to save the person, but rather to be a hero, then he or she acted immorally even if the person is ultimately saved. The reason why the deontologist would say the medical student acted immorally is because the medical student used the person as a means to be seen as a hero and did not respect the person for his own sake in attempting to save him. If the person called with the intention to save the person, but the person died anyway, he or she acted morally, since the person's death was not in the medical student's control.

To summarize the deontological framework:

1. One's duty is not based on one's personal goals or what is outside of one's control.
2. One's duty is based on what one can do in a situation and what anyone who is in that situation who has the same abilities should do.
3. Moral action means fulfilling one's duty because it is the moral thing to do, and not because it serves a different goal or purpose.

Consequentialist (utilitarian) ethics

From a consequentialist perspective, the moral worth of any action is based on the measure of goodness that the action produces. The best action is the one that will bring about the best outcome for everyone involved. How that outcome is achieved and the intentions one has in being motivated to act matter only as part of the calculation of what happens. By relying on future outcomes, however, consequentialism faces two challenges. First, it is difficult to define what should be considered "good" and what constitutes the "best" outcome. For example, consequentialists can disagree whether their goal should be (a) to spread happiness and relieve suffering, or (b) to create as much freedom or choice as possible in the world, or (c) to promote the survival of our species. Second, any alternative has only a probability of success, and there might be unforeseen consequences as well. Therefore, determining which alternative is best faces the difficulty both of how to define what is best and how to determine the effectiveness of each choice.

The most common form of consequentialism is utilitarianism, which defines the good in terms of happiness. Utilitarianism utilizes what is known as the greatest happiness principle – which means that the best action will achieve the greatest happiness for the greatest number of people. By allowing for one standard of measure – happiness – utilitarianism avoids any possibility of moral dilemma. All one has to do is reduce every option to the common currency of happiness, and pick the option which maximizes the benefit.

The most basic form of utilitarianism is "act utilitarianism" which posits that the morally right action to choose is the one that achieves the greatest happiness as a consequence of that choice. Within act utilitarianism, however, there are, nevertheless, two ways of evaluating different alternatives. The first is to say that the act that causes the best consequences is the only right option, and all others are wrong. The second is to say that the act that causes the best consequences is better than the alternatives, commensurate with the greater benefit, but the alternatives are not wrong per se.

"Rule utilitarianism" is a more nuanced form of utilitarianism, since it considers the effect of generalizing a particular act and evaluating the consequences when the act becomes a common practice. Therefore, a rule consequentialist would posit that an action is morally right if it conforms to a rule that leads to the greatest good. If the rule by which the considered act conforms would not lead to the greatest good, the act should not be done. For example, in a case where a patient asks for an antibiotic for a virus, an act utilitarian might argue that giving her the antibiotic would be a good decision, provided that it does not hurt her and will give her possible benefits through the placebo effect or from the pleasure she gets knowing her request was granted. However, a rule utilitarian would argue that if everyone who asks for unnecessary treatment of an antibiotic received one, there would be great negative consequences, in terms of creating resistant strains and wasting resources. A rule utilitarian would therefore not agree to say that providing the antibiotic would be a good choice.

In the field of medical ethics, consequentialist calculations are most often and explicitly applied in cases where there are limited resources and one needs to figure out who to treat and who not to treat in a relatively timely manner. Principles used in cases of triage are a good example of when consequentialist frames are applied to medical ethics decision-making – in triage, one sorts and allocates treatment to patients according to a system of priorities designed to maximize the number of survivors.

Value(s) comparison between deontology and consequentialism

As mentioned above, deontology and consequentialism are the two major moral philosophies that people use today when deliberating on how one should act in situations regarding medical and general ethics, and, while a few moral philosophers have attempted to show how they converge, "climbing the same ethical mountain on different sides,"[13] for most ethicists the differences in the values the two moral philosophies prioritize provide good examples of how frames and biases affect ethical decision-making. These differences should not persuade you to think that you can simply pick the frame that best suits your initial gut reactions or desires and use ethical thinking as a tool for rationalization. On the contrary, relying on the premise that you actually want to act on your values, when deliberating on a moral decision, you should use the different moral philosophies as ways to analyze your reasoning and to judge how different moral frames influence your decision. When you find that different frameworks come up with different conclusions, you should try to understand which values each philosophy prioritizes and which each de-emphasizes, so that you might find alternatives that you might not otherwise consider.

Below are three examples where deontological conclusions differ from consequentialist ones. The first example is in providing cardiopulmonary resuscitation (CPR) to a person in the hospital whose heart stopped and there is a low but real chance that you could save her, but in doing so, you would cause her pain and physical harm. Depending on how one measures the value (in terms of her and others' happiness) of her survival, a consequentialist may offer that it would be a better decision to do nothing than to try to save her, since, in either case, the probability is that the woman would die, but in attempting to save her you will cause her additional pain. According to the deontologist, however, you should try to save her, since you should consider the possibility that she might die, despite your efforts, to be out of your control. For you, the moral duty would be to try to save her. For consequentialists, the outcome matters; for deontologists, a person's intention to fulfill his or her duty matters.

The second example pertains to defensive medicine. Defensive medicine occurs when a doctor recommends a diagnostic test or medical treatment that is not necessarily the best option for the patient. It mainly serves to protect the physician against a potential malpractice lawsuit. If practicing defensive medicine results in improving health care as a whole, then a consequentialist would say that it is a good decision, despite the intentions. A deontologist, however, would say that because the intention is to protect the physician from a lawsuit and not to help the patient, defensive medicine is not morally justified.

Finally, there is the trolley case, originally proposed by Philippa Foot. In the trolley case, there is a runaway trolley barreling down the railway tracks. Ahead, on the tracks, there are five people tied up and unable to move. The trolley is headed straight for them. Imagine you are standing some distance off in the train yard, next to a lever. If you pull this lever, the trolley will switch to a different set of tracks.

However, you notice that there is one person on the other set of tracks. You have two options:

1. Do nothing, and the trolley kills the five people on the main track.
2. Pull the lever, diverting the trolley onto the side track where it will kill one person.

To make the trolley case relevant to medical ethics, consider the following parallel case: There is a person in a persistent vegetative state on a ventilator and any medical treatment would be considered futile. There are eight people who can be saved if the person in the persistent vegetative state donates his organs to those people, and they will die if the person does not. You have two options:

1. Kill the person, recover his organs and save the eight people.
2. Do not recover his organs and the other eight people will die.

The medical ethics case should be seen as strictly theoretical, since legally a person must be dead before his organs can be recovered and there are currently no medical professional societies that endorse killing patients.[14] The case could be made more realistic, and complicated, by assuming that the person has an organ donor card, is brain dead, yet in a state that also respects people's choice to determine death according to cardiopulmonary criteria rather than neurological criteria, and that there is a doubt whether the patient condones brain death as a valid definition of death or not, but that would add too many factors into the moral equation and cloud the differences between the two moral frameworks. Noting these additional factors, however, does allow us to recognize that even seemingly analogous cases may be very different when considering all of the medical and social details of particular cases.

For a consequentialist, in both cases, saving more people is a better outcome than saving one person. Moreover, just as in the trolley case where the consequentialist would pull the lever, so too in the medical ethics case the consequentialist would make the argument that killing the one patient in a persistent vegetative state to save eight would be the best option, since it would produce the best consequences. The deontologist, however, would argue that killing is categorically wrong. Therefore, regardless of the consequences, one should not kill someone to save others. Just as in the trolley case where the deontologist would not pull the lever; in the medical ethics case, if the other eight people die before the patient dies, it may be unfortunate, but saving them is not in one's control.

In real life, however, people are not strictly consequentialists or deontologists, and oftentimes, people have contradictory responses if slight changes to a scenario are made. For example, in the trolley case, a pure consequentialist would not change his or her response if, instead of pulling a lever, he or she would have to throw a person on the tracks to derail the train and save the five people. In either case, he would be willing to sacrifice one to save five. However, Joshua Greene has shown through experimentation that when asked about the two scenarios, most people would feel more comfortable killing someone indirectly through pulling a lever than directly by throwing them in front of a train.[15] When people make these types of distinctions in the trolley case, it means that they either:

1. think that consequentialism is incomplete,
2. have certain biases that they have incorporated, or
3. are using different moral frameworks in coming to each decision.

The trolley case, therefore, provides an excellent example in how different moral philosophies frame ethical scenarios, given the value premises that underlie them. Moreover, given that most people change how they view the ethical question when asked about resolving the challenge directly rather than indirectly, the case also provides a good example of how people think about ethical challenges differently when they consider the question, "what should be done," in contrast to the question, "if I were to act on my values, how would I act in this case." For the sake both of making moral decisions and acting on those decisions, the trolley case, therefore, provides two important lessons. First, when thinking about which values you want to voice, you should not see the various ethical frameworks as computational formulae, where you put in a question and let the framework spit out an answer. Rather, you should think about how the ethical frameworks prioritize values differently and how they might help you think about how to prioritize the different, and sometimes conflicting, values that you have which are affected by a particular case at hand. In this way, the different moral philosophies should give you different strategies for thinking, just like the GVV methodology imparts the importance of thinking about different strategies for acting. Second, when thinking about how to act so that your values are voiced, visualizing how you will implement the decision directly is an important part of weighing whether the moral decision you made is realistic in practice, given your value premises and your own assumptions about yourself. We will discuss this more in the next chapter, when we look at personal–professional profiles.

Principlism or the Four Principles approach

This is the ethical framework that has been developed specifically in the context of medical ethics. Principlism, or the Four Principles approach to medical ethics, identifies four basic moral principles as the starting points for practical decision-making. The four principles are: (1) respect for autonomy, (2) non-maleficence, (3) beneficence, and (4) justice. In thinking about a medical ethics case, a person would balance the four principles in light of the goals of medicine to make a proper moral decision. Beauchamp and Childress, two philosophers who devised this approach, offer six conditions that should be met when trying to balance the four principles:

1. Good reasons can be offered to prioritize one principle over another.
2. The choice which prioritizes one principle over another is realistically achievable.
3. There are no preferable alternatives.
4. The choice made attempts to achieve the highest demonstration of each principle; any other choice would provide a lower valuation of one of the principles. (This condition is meant to avoid prioritizing autonomy indiscriminately.)
5. Negative consequences have been minimized.
6. All affected parties have been treated impartially.[16]

It might seem like Principlism is just another form of consequentialism since it focuses on minimizing negative consequences and maximizing positive ones, and that the difference between utilitarian and Principlism is that the former attempts to maximize one value, i.e. that of happiness, while Principlism attempts to balance four so as to maximize each without taking away from any other.

One criticism of Principlism is that each of the four principles are inherently vague and potentially subjective. Think of our discussion of autonomy above; it can either be seen as simply not interfering with patients or incorporating the duty for physicians to raise the level of understanding and the capabilities of patients. Similarly, beneficence means to do good, yet conflicting priorities and the plurality of definitions for what constitutes the good disallows such a simple understanding. For example, the goods of medicine comprise preserving life, promoting health, relieving suffering, and curing disease, and each person may have different ways of prioritizing them, if not adding to them. Therefore, the benefit of using Principlism when deliberating on medical ethics cases is more in the way that it might demand that you define your terms and provide ways to show that your definitions can apply in practice. It can also help you think about whether you are prioritizing your values fairly and thoughtfully in situations where they might be in conflict.

Notes

1 Gerd Gigerenzer defines a gut reaction as a judgment that (1) appear quickly in consciousness, yet (2) the person is not aware of the underlying reasons for the judgment, but (3) the judgment is strong enough for the person to act upon it. (Gigerenzer, G. (2007). *Gut Feelings: The Intelligence of the Unconscious*. Penguin, 16.)

2 Halpern, J. (2001). *From Detached Concern to Empathy: Humanizing Medical Practice*. Oxford University Press, 3.

3 Abbott, A. (2016). Modern Milgram experiment sheds light on power of authority. *Nature, 530*, 394–395.

4 Burger, J. M. (2014). Situational features in Milgram's experiment that kept his participants shocking. *Journal of Social Issues, 70*(3), 489–500.

5 www.acog.org/Clinical-Guidance-and-Publications/Committee-Opinions/Committee-on-Ethics/Professional-Responsibilities-in-Obstetric-Gynecologic-Medical-Education-and-Training

6 This means that a patient is able to freely decline a physician who is assigned to them; the patient–physician relationship does not begin until the patient agrees to see a

particular doctor. Similarly, when a patient schedules an appointment, he or she is offering to enter into a contractual relationship with the physician. Only when the physician engages with the patient, by taking a history or examining him or her, does the physician accept the offer and a contract is formed. Before this time, the doctor may reject the offer and refuse to treat him or her. There is no legal obligation for a physician to accept a patient if he or she does not want to do so. The voluntariness of a physician not to accept a patient, however, is only justified when the reason is not prohibited by contract or by law. For example, the Civil Rights Act of 1964 prohibits physicians that receive federal funding, including Medicare and Medicaid, from discriminating against patients on the basis of race, color, religion, or national origin. Based on the interpretation of the Supreme Court, this ruling includes discrimination on the basis of language, thereby including patients with Limited English Proficiency. Also, the Americans with Disabilities Act prohibits discrimination against patients with disabilities, including patients with HIV/AIDS or anyone who has a known association or relationship with an individual who has HIV. Similarly, physicians cannot discriminate based on sexual orientation. This dynamic reflects the contract nature of the patient–physician relationship. Hospitals, on the other hand, must by law provide emergency treatment to anyone who comes to the emergency department. If the hospital does not have the capability to treat the condition, it must make an "appropriate" transfer of the patient to another hospital with such capability.

7 A fiduciary is a person who is engaged in a legal or ethical relationship, where the person is entrusted to act in the best interests of another person.

8 Beneficence means that physicians act for the benefit of others. Non-maleficence means that physicians seek to avoid harming others.

9 Medical paternalism occurs when a physician directs the care of a patient, even with the intent of promoting his or her good, without the patient's consent.

10 Patrick, V. M., & Hagtvedt; H. (2012). "I don't" versus "I can't": When empowered refusal motivates goal-directed behavior. *Journal of Consumer Research, 39*(2), 371–381.

11 For example, moral egoism is the normative ethical position that people ought to do what is in their own self-interest. This is different from psychological egoism, the claim that people can only act in their self-interest.

12 Even for those who think that morality is relative, meaning that there is no objective right and wrong but rather that moral judgments are only relative to some particular standpoint, with none that is better than any other, moral relativists should still be able to assert that within a particular standpoint, there are norms and values which guide moral decision-making.

13 This expression is adapted from the one used by Derek Parfitt, in *On What Matters: Volume One*. In this three-volume work, Parfitt attempts to show how deontology, consequentialism, and contractualism can be reconciled.

14 See, however, the article citation below by Michael Nair Collins, who argues that the bright line that separates brain death from all other conditions for clinical and legal purposes is not justified by any morally relevant distinctions. Nair-Collins, M. (2017). Can the brain-dead be harmed or wronged?: On the moral status of brain death and its implications for organ transplantation. *Kennedy Institute of Ethics Journal, 27*(4), 525–559.

15 Greene, J. D., Cushman, F. A., Stewart, L. E., Lowenberg, K., Nystrom, L. E., & Cohen, J. D. (2009). Pushing moral buttons: The interaction between personal force and intention in moral judgment. *Cognition, 111*(3), 364–371.

16 Childress, J. F., & Beauchamp, T. L. (2009). *Principles of Biomedical Ethics*. Oxford University Press, USA, 23.

3

ACTING ON MORAL DECISIONS

Moral (in)action: Rationalizations check

While the GVV methodology incorporates a post-decision method to create strategies for efficacious moral action, when faced in the future with a choice to act, you should first consider whether the choice that you make in fact allows you to voice your values or whether you are providing rationalizations for not voicing them. Learning whether your decisions rationalize inaction or whether they lead you to do what you want to do will also help you respond to the rationalizations that you will encounter from others who do not want to implement your decision.

The process of explaining one's desired actions can occur in one of two ways, either one starts with premises or values which one uses to reach a conclusion, or one starts with a conclusion and then finds ways to justify it. Starting with your premises or values leads to reasoning while starting with the conclusion leads to rationalization. Sometimes people begin to rationalize without even realizing they are doing so. This can occur when they are so committed to their gut reaction that any further deliberation is simply a means to justify why their gut reaction should be followed rather than thinking about whether their gut reaction is correct or not. This can also happen when people's perceptions or emotional biases prevent them from thinking about the situation from different perspectives or make people unable to see if there are other facts or values to consider. Another way rationalization occurs unconsciously is when people have already internalized the idea that they do not have the power, authority, or ability to raise concerns or voice their values. In this situation, it is not that people have not given thought to whether they are in fact appropriately applying their values; rather, they have accepted the notion that they are unable to do so, and have begun to justify why they shouldn't act. In situations like these, if people felt that they could in fact voice their values and that action were possible, they would begin ethical deliberation and strategizing from a very different starting point and perspective.

The difference between rationalizing and reasoning are typically seen in the fact that explanations that seek to do the former focus on motivations for acting, or, better, not acting, while the latter focus on how to best act. In other words, if the explanation for your choice provides an answer to why you want to act a certain way or not, then the explanation is probably a rationalization. If, on the other hand, the explanation for your choice presumes that the choice is based on your values and is, therefore, seeking to explain why this choice is the best alternative, then the explanation is probably a reason for acting in a particular way. For example, giving the answer "this is common practice" to explain why to continue a course of action does not speak as to whether the practice is in line with your own values or not. On the other hand, the answer "the common practice is the best way to ensure I …" does. Of course, this is just a rule of thumb, but it could serve as a helpful heuristic to test yourself.

Personal–professional profiles

When thinking about how best to act on your values, the first and primary factor that you should consider is yourself. Yet, considering yourself in this way is not self-centeredness; rather, it is with the intent to act in a way that is conducive to who you are. Polonius's last words to his son Laertes, "to thine own self be true,"[1] means more than simply knowing what is in one's best interests or, for the sake of moral action, knowing what is best for oneself. In the GVV methodology, it also means knowing your own strengths and preferences so that when acting on your own values, you can do so in a way that builds on your unique strengths rather than against them. Self-knowledge becomes the medium by which self-image is cast and, in this way, professional identity formation becomes a way to shape what one already possesses as opposed to working with a *tabula rasa*.

At this starting point for moral action, we can assume that part of your self-knowledge includes the first two starting assumptions of the GVV method. First, you want to voice and act on your values, and second, you have voiced your values at some point in the past. Examining your experience in acting on your values in the past, you can consider not only what strategies worked and which did not, given a particular situation, but also what motivated *you* to act and what strategies were more comfortable *for you* to implement. For example, some people are motivated by the idea that they like to take risks or be seen as contrarian. Those people might be motivated to act because they see a situation where they can embody that self-view. Others are motivated by the fear of violating moral norms or legal/professional codes. Those who see themselves in this way may also speak up in the same situation as those who see themselves as more contrarian, albeit for a very different reason. Rather than seeing themselves as individuals speaking against the norm, they will see themselves as speaking towards it. For both of these types of individuals who may be motivated to speak up, not only will they have different motivating factors, the strategies that they might use will be different as well. They might also recognize the need to seek out allies and partners. For example, the contrarian might recognize that a given situation calls for a deferential response and may therefore seek out someone who can help him or her find the way to approach the right channels of authority, while the more risk-averse person might realize that he or she needs someone more courageous to join the effort. As one can see, successful action does not entail a one size fits all approach, each person must recognize what they bring to a successful strategy and what they are not comfortable doing (based on their own personal strengths and demeanors, not out of moral judgment), so that they can find the right collaborators to help them when needed.

Knowing your own strengths and preferences will allow you to construct a personal–professional profile. This profile will help you determine what you can do comfortably to implement your action plan and for what you might need assistance so that your plan can be successful without having to change your identity. The personal–professional profile should not be seen as a way to justify typecasting yourself or to rationalize the belief that self-growth is not possible or important. Trying new skills and experiences will let you build a broader sense of self. However, the profile does let you recognize that at the time of action there are just certain things that you may not be able to do even if you might be able to do them in the future. This allows you to be real with yourself so that your action plan is based on honest assumptions. In thinking about your personal–professional profile, there are no right or wrong answers to who you are. Everyone is unique in having their own set of skills, passions, and dispositions. Knowing who you are is the goal of the exercise, not comparing yourself to anyone else. Mary Gentile, in her book, *Giving Voice to Values: How to Speak Your Mind When You Know What's Right*, provides a list of self-assessment questions which are helpful in constructing your personal–professional profile. An adaptation of some of her key assessment questions are as follows.[2]

Questions of personal purpose

- What are your personal goals?
- What are your professional goals?
- What impact do you want to make through your work? On whom?
- How do you define your impact as a physician?
- What will make your professional life worthwhile?
- How do you feel about yourself and your work, both while you are engaged in it and as a professional and personal goal?

Questions of risk

- Are you risk averse or a risk taker?
- What are the greatest risks you face as a medical student? As a physician? Are these personal (livelihood, legal, social, familial), professional (harm to patients, colleagues), or societal (impact on profession, communities)?
- What level of risk are you comfortable taking?

Questions of personal communication style and preference

- Are you comfortable with confrontation or no?
- Do you prefer communicating in person or in writing?
- Do you respond best in the moment or after time has passed?
- Do you assert your position with statements or communicate through asking pointed questions?

Questions of loyalty

- Do you tend to feel the greatest loyalty to family, colleagues, your employer, or other stakeholders, such as patients?
- How do different conditions and different stakes affect your sense of loyalty?

Questions of self-image

- Generally speaking, do you consider yourself astute or naïve?
- Do you identify as idealistic, opportunistic, pragmatic, or a combination of all three (in what degrees)? Remember, none of these should be seen with moral judgment, they are simply three different ways of engaging or responding to an opportunity or a challenge.
- Are you more comfortable as a learner or a teacher?
- Are you more comfortable as an autonomous individual contributor or as a member of a collaborative team?
- Can you think of a situation where you surprised yourself? What surprised you? What may have been different about the situation that made you see something different about yourself?

When going through the cases at the end of the book, you should think about the personal–professional profiles of the protagonists as well as your own personal–professional profile. This will allow you to create strategies and scripts that are realistic for developing your own skills and plans for moral action in the future.

Considering other stakeholders

From an interprofessional perspective, consider not only your own roles and responsibilities on the collaborative care team, but also the roles, goals, and responsibilities of the other members. Consider what you can do yourself and your limitations in assuming or delegating tasks, and accept responsibility for how you can impact the team. Think about which members of the team might share your values and would be open to implementing the choice you would want to enact, as well as which members would not be. Think also about what is at stake for the different members of the team if they were to join you in implementing your action plan. Are there any personal or professional risks to them that you can mitigate? How would the different ways of approaching the various stakeholders impact them emotionally, which might affect whether they join you or not?

Also, many times, other members of the collaborative care team will have much more experience working in the system than you. Therefore, they may know more effective ways to reach the desired choice of action, and they can be a valuable resource for you. Moreover, different members of the team may have stronger relationships with each other and/or with the patient. They may thus be better spokespeople to help persuade the different stakeholders in a given situation. However, this does not mean that there would be nothing for you to do in that situation. Rather, it means that you should try to engage those people to work with you in developing an effective action plan and/or script so that your values are voiced. Especially in healthcare, clinical and ethical action should always be seen as a collaborative endeavor, so asking others for assistance should be seen as a strength.

Organizational and systems-based levers

From an organizational and systems perspective, relevant laws, professional societies' policy statements, and the hospital policies regarding the issue(s) at hand will not only let you understand how similar situations were confronted and regulated in the past, but they can also be used as levers to help influence others to implement your action plan. This does not mean that you should simply defer to these norms. Rather, in looking at these norms, you should determine whether the moral challenge you face is one of non-compliance of the team, differing value premises, or misunderstanding of the situation. If the laws, policy statements, and hospital policies are in line with your decision, they become strong support in persuading others. If they do not, then you may have to determine whether you disagree with the values that the greater professional and legal culture upholds or whether you have not thought of all of the ramifications of your decision. If the former, then your strategy or script must confront a larger tide; if the latter, then you might have to reconsider your decision.

It is also important to consider the cultural and socio-economic backgrounds of various stakeholders, especially patients. When choosing a particular strategy that demands patients' compliance, an alternative that does not take into account the ability of patients to comply with that strategy, whether it be for cultural, religious, or socioeconomic reasons, will not be successful. For example, suggesting a particular treatment plan that will not be covered by a person's insurance and the person has no other way to pay for it might put undue stress on the patient for the sake of one's own personal values. This might not be the best alternative to pursue. There may be other alternatives that can limit the demands on others while still being in line with one's own values.

There is no single way to carry out a decision, but there are better and worse ways to do so. The best strategies for action are those that are in line with your values and personal–professional profile, consider the other people involved, and where you have devised means for implementation given the organizational environment. Knowing how you can act given the environment in which you want to voice your values is as important as knowing which values you want to voice.

Creating scripts

When developing a script to talk to other members of the collaborative care team, to the patient, and to the patient's family, anticipate how your words will be received, interpreted, and accepted. From the perspective of talking to patients, even if you think that you are giving authoritative guidance, you can project an authoritarian posture through your communication style. For example, if a physician uses technical terms and medical jargon that the patient does not understand, he or she may be projecting the idea that the physician is in charge and the patient must simply comply since he or she does not understand enough to contribute. Similarly, if the physician interrupts a patient, he or she may be conveying the idea that the patient's words are irrelevant. Tone is also sometimes more value-laden than content, since it provides information about one's level of attention and motivations that words can only do incompletely. Tone relies more on body language and verbal cues than words alone and is also subject to interpretation to a greater degree than words are. When talking with a patient, be cognizant not only of the words you use, but also in how you use them. Also, pay attention to how the patient receives your questions and what his or her body language is telling you. Patients consider not only the medical competence of the physician but also his or her attitude and perceived intentions. Like any social interaction, when a patient and physician communicate with each other, they also influence each other's perspectives and emotional states, both consciously and unconsciously. If one side is friendly and open to conversing, the other will be more willing to open up as well. If one side is rude or dismissive, the other will begin to close him- or herself off. Moreover, when physicians engage in patient-centered communication, such as in asking questions and providing guidance, patients perceive that their physician's medical skill is higher than when he or she simply gives directions, and will be more prone to accepting a physician's suggestions.[3]

Keep in mind that different people understand terms in different ways, which may help or hinder what one wants to accomplish. For example, among themselves, physicians understand the term "futility" and use it without any judgment of the patient, since the term connotes the lack of efficacy of different treatment alternatives. However, patients hear the term futility to mean "not worth trying" which creates a disconnect between the physician and the patient. In cases where treatment might be futile, physicians should consider using other terms, such as medically non-beneficial or even saying that a treatment will not accomplish the medical goals that both the patient and the physician seek. Also, many times a patient will not ask a physician to repeat or explain an unfamiliar term, so physicians must be sensitive to the words they use and not assume that patients understand them.

From the interprofessional perspective, because different professionals emphasize different aspects of care and use different jargon or ways of discussing patient care, you will need to think about how to communicate with other members of the team. This includes not only seeking clarification in a respectful manner when misunderstandings arise, but also communicating in ways that other team members can understand. It also includes providing persuasive responses to the reasons or rationalizations that other professionals may have in response to your decision, as well as allowing for "give and take" so that others can voice their opinions or pertinent views in a process that allows for collaborative decision-making rather than asserting overt pressure. For example, nurses oftentimes speak about patients by way of longer narratives that include psychosocial factors and the patient's illness experience, while some physicians tend to focus on pathologies and treatments. As such, when trying to include either other physicians or nurses to help implement your plan, consider how others will hear that plan so as to be persuasive.

When communicating with both patients and other healthcare professionals, as important as finding the right words is your ability to listen and consider others' views of both medical and personal goals so that they can be addressed. This requires active listening techniques, unambiguous language, and structured questioning to allow others, patients and members of the collaborative care team included, to reach their own conclusions as well as understand your views from their own perspective.

Notes

1 *Hamlet*, Act 1, scene 3.
2 pp. 116–117.
3 Haddad, S., Potvin, L., Roberge, D., Pineault, R., & Remondin, M. (2000). Patient perception of quality following a visit to a doctor in a primary care unit. *Family Practice, 17*(1), 21–29.

4

CASES

Case 1: Confronting a superior

Assignment

In this case, you will read about Maria, a second-year resident, who decides to confront a neonatology fellow about using local anesthesia when inserting a chest tube in a newborn. After reading the case presentation and discussion, prepare an action plan and script for Maria's conversation with the fellow.

- You are not given Maria's complete personal–professional profile in the case description. Before preparing your action plan and script for Maria, please create a personal–professional profile for her and think about how her personal–professional profile affects the emotional impact the case has on her both positively and negatively. Also, consider how her profile shapes which action strategy would be most effective.
- Your action strategy should include plans for gathering the additional information she might need, identifying and approaching allies who may be helpful, recognizing and utilizing any opportunities that may be available, identifying and mitigating any challenges that she might foresee, and crafting alternative solutions that incorporate these factors.
- In preparing your script, consider not only her own perspective, but also the perspective of the neonatology fellow. Think about the actual words you would have her say and how her words will be heard by the neonatology fellow, as well as how the fellow might respond. Your script should incorporate the rationalizations or responses that you anticipate the fellow voicing and how Maria can reply to them. As such, the "script" should be more like a decision-tree than a monologue.

- Remember that the ethical question in this case is not simply what Maria would do for herself, but how well she can act on her own values in light of her patient's goals and her ability to act on them successfully.
- Refer to the rubric and be sure to include all elements listed when creating your script and in preparing for your explanation for why you came up with your script and action strategy.

Case presentation

One day, when Maria was a second-year pediatrics resident, working in the neonatal intensive care unit (NICU), she was assigned to care for a full-term baby boy, who was born by cesarean section and came to the unit for respiratory distress. The infant was diagnosed with transient tachypnea of newborn (TTN), which occurs when a newborn breathes more rapidly than normal. The condition, which occurs more often after births by cesarean section than vaginal births, is caused by the obstruction of the lungs' air sacs (alveoli) by residual amniotic fluid that remains in the newborn's lungs after delivery. It is usually transient and many babies with TTN will get better on their own because each breath they take pulls more air into the lungs, expands the alveoli, and pushes the excess fluid out. The fluid is then either coughed out or it gets reabsorbed through the capillaries in the lungs. This baby, though, did not get better on his own, but rather he got worse. His respiratory distress persisted and he was ultimately placed on nasal CPAP (continuous positive airway pressure through small tubes in his nose), which helped to keep his airways open while still allowing him to breathe on his own.

Over the course of the next few days, the infant developed pneumothoraces (accumulations of air between the lungs and the chest wall), which is a known potential complication of CPAP. The air accumulated between his lungs and chest wall was putting pressure on his lungs and preventing them from filling up completely, making it more difficult for the infant to breathe despite the CPAP. The attending physician determined that the infant needed to have a chest tube to remove the air trapped between his lungs and chest wall so as to improve his respiratory distress. He ordered that Maria assist the neonatology fellow in inserting the chest tube. A fellow is someone who has more advanced training than a resident, but is not yet a neonatology attending physician. In order to place a chest tube, a physician creates a small incision through the infant's skin and muscle, in the space between two of his ribs. Then a narrow tube is inserted through the hole into the space between the lung and the chest wall. The tube is then securely sutured to the skin with one or two stitches, and the end is attached to a machine with suction so that the air is drawn out from the space. This ultimately allows the infant's lungs to fully inflate.

The neonatology fellow told Maria to get ready to place the chest tube as she would supervise her in doing it. As she set off to collect the supplies, Maria asked the fellow about anesthesia or sedation for the baby. The fellow responded, "He doesn't need anything. The procedure will be fast." The response surprised Maria for several reasons. First, Maria had experience in inserting chest tubes in adult patients, and remembered using local anesthesia. Second, she had been taught that infants also experience pain during invasive procedures. Maria did not know the hospital policy for using local anesthetics on infants, but as she continued gathering the supplies, she asked one of the nurses what usually is done, and she said that they usually apply a local anesthetic on the area before inserting the tube. Though Maria had a lot of respect for the fellow's judgment and it was her first time involved in a procedure like this for infants, she did not want to do the procedure without first giving the newborn anesthesia, knowing that it would cause the newborn pain. She decided to raise her concerns with the fellow in order to persuade her that they should use local anesthesia. In deciding to raise her concerns, Maria would need to think about who the various stakeholders are and what was at stake for them, as well as how she could raise her concern and still maintain a stable working relationship with the fellow.

Discussion: Who are the key stakeholders and what is at stake for them?

In this situation, the main stakeholders would be the infant, Maria, the fellow, and the infant's parents. The infant would experience unnecessary pain if Maria inserted the chest tube without first applying local anesthetic. Maria wants to act on her values, which consists of more than just avoiding harm or pain for her patients, she also does not want to be the type of person who inflicts or causes pain to someone else unnecessarily. Yet, she also does not want to sacrifice her relationship with the fellow. The fellow might not want to be disrespected or appear incompetent or unknowledgeable in front of a resident or the other members of the collaborative care team, let alone the attending. Therefore, any approach that Maria takes in confronting her would have to be sensitive to the hierarchical relationship between herself and the fellow and thoughtful as to how the fellow might hear Maria's concerns. Also, in order to insert the chest tube, the fellow and Maria would have to explain to the infant's parents the nature of the procedure and reasons for administering it in order to obtain their informed consent. While the parents might not ask if the procedure will be painful, the possibility that such a question might be raised can provide an opportunity to discuss the issue with the fellow. If the parents find out that Maria and the fellow did not use a local anesthetic when inserting the chest tube, and that the child experienced pain unnecessarily, their relationship with the medical team might be weakened.

Additional stakeholders could be other members of the healthcare team and the hospital. The attending physician, who has ultimate responsibility for the care of this patient, would be accountable for anything that Maria or the fellow did that did not meet the proper standard of care. Moreover, the other members of the team and the hospital could also be hurt, either directly or indirectly, by any improper actions that Maria or the fellow performed.

Can you think of any other stakeholders? Can you think of what else might be at stake?

What arguments or rationalizations is Maria likely to encounter?

We already saw that the fellow responded to Maria's initial question about anesthesia with, "He doesn't need anything." If probed further, Maria may be forcing the fellow either to admit that she was wrong or to continue to rationalize why she believes the infant does not need an anesthetic. The former alternative creates a situation of conflict and the latter alternative creates a situation of defensiveness as well as pain for the infant.

The fellow could also simply say that she was in charge, and thus Maria needed to follow her instructions. This would be a demand to be obedient to authority, which does not have ethical justification in this situation. Alternatively, she could say "We never give anesthesia for these procedures." In this case, she could try to sway Maria by implying that it is acceptable practice because it is what everyone does. However, that argument has nothing to do with ethical reasoning. It is a common rationalization called "standard practice." Standard practice implies that a person's actions are acceptable because others would do the same thing. This assumption assumes that the ethical value of an action is based on the number of people who engage in the action, yet this has no moral foundation. In fact, this argument could be used even to justify harmful actions, such as the one in this case, namely, doing a painful procedure without anesthesia. In this case, the rationalization that not using anesthesia is standard practice is actually inaccurate.

The fellow may also argue that the injection of the local anesthetic might cause pain as well. Maria could offer the alternative of using a topical anesthetic if it were possible, or she could respond by saying that the pain the baby will feel when injecting the anesthesia would be less than the pain of inserting the chest tube and sutures without it.

Can you think of other rationalizations that the fellow may offer?

What strategies can Maria use to counter the fellow's arguments and plot a course of action for addressing the situation?

In the process of developing a strategy, Maria should consider various factors such as what is at stake for the different stakeholders, the communication style she uses and the location where she decides to raise her concerns, the availability of information and data, the complexity of the situation, and risk.

Audience

Maria should be aware of her current relationship with the fellow, and be aware how the fellow might take her concerns. Maria should recognize both the authority and the experience of the fellow, and pose her concerns in a way that shows respect to her colleague.

If Maria were to include the nurse with whom she spoke or the attending, she may cause the fellow to feel that Maria caused her to look incompetent or unknowledgeable, which would hurt their professional relationship. If she brought up the use of a local anesthetic while in front of the parents, it may cause conflict between the medical team and the parents at a time when the parents are already in an emotional state.

Communication style and location

This is a conversation to have in person and in private. Maria's communication style should make it clear that she respects the fellow and is not questioning the fellow's general medical knowledge or integrity. Maria should make clear, however, that the fellow should consider her concerns and not simply dismiss them as questions for personal edification but rather meant for the best interests of the infant as well as to promote her own professional integrity.

Availability of information and data

To avoid any of the rationalizations that the fellow may give, Maria should be prepared with either the professional or hospital policy guidelines regarding the use of local anesthetics when inserting chest tubes in infants. She should also discretely become aware what the standard practice actually is in the hospital and the reasons behind that policy. She can also pose to the fellow how the fellow might explain the procedure to the infant's parents and how she would tell them about the decision whether to use local anesthesia or not. By asking this question, Maria is also letting the fellow know that she should be bringing the issue up to the infant's parents. By posing questions to the fellow, Maria can use her manner of actively listening to the fellow's responses as a way to clarify, probe, and have both her and the fellow reflect on each other's position.

Complexity of the situation

While the nature of the situation is relatively straightforward in terms of the decision to apply local anesthesia, the working relationship between colleagues, and between those in authority–subordinate relationships, is at times complex. This demands that Maria's strategy balances the tension between respecting the authority of the fellow and persuading the fellow to change her mind about using local anesthesia.

Risks

The most obvious risk is that of the working relationship between Maria and the fellow. If handled incorrectly, not only will the infant experience unnecessary pain, but the fellow may no longer want to work with Maria anymore. The fellow may also speak negatively about Maria to others and give Maria a bad evaluation.

Potential strategy

Once Maria considers these factors, she can begin to develop a plan to raise her concerns with the fellow. One potential strategy to apply in this case would be for Maria to take a "learning stance" where she asks the fellow questions about her initial response in a way that demonstrates Maria's desire to understand the fellow's decision better. In taking a learning stance, Maria can ask the fellow what the differences are between pain thresholds for adults and children, as well as what the hospital or professional policies are for the different patient populations. She can also ask how will they inform the parents about not using local anesthesia when obtaining informed consent for this procedure. In this way, Maria is not challenging the fellow directly, since the learning stance is not confrontation or adversarial, but rather acknowledges the fellow's authority and experience. In this way, Maria can give voice to her concerns in a way that does not put the fellow on the defensive. It might even allow for the fellow to come to Maria's suggestion on her own.

How can Maria reframe the matter in a conversation with the fellow? What should she say and what support should she or should she not utilize?

Case 2: HIV mothers and breastfeeding their newborns

Assignment

In this case, you will read about Dr. Delgado, an OBGYN, who helps Roberta deliver her baby, Thomas. Roberta who is HIV positive wants to breastfeed Thomas, and Dr. Delgado decides to speak to her about not doing so. After reading the case presentation and discussion, prepare an action plan and script for Dr. Delgado's conversation with Roberta.

- You are not given Dr. Delgado's complete personal–professional profile in the case description. Before preparing your action plan and script for Dr. Delgado, please create a personal–professional profile for her and think about how her personal–professional profile affects the emotional impact the case has on her both positively and negatively. Also, consider how her profile shapes which action strategy would be most effective.
- Your action strategy should include plans for gathering the additional information she might need, identifying and approaching allies who may be helpful (including which other medical professionals might be helpful to include in your strategy, what their roles might be, and what resources they may have which can help implement your plan successfully), recognizing and utilizing any opportunities that may be available, identifying and mitigating any challenges that she might foresee, and crafting alternative solutions that incorporate these factors.
- In preparing your script, consider not only Dr. Delgado's own perspective, but also Roberta's perspective. Think about the actual words you would

have Dr. Delgado say and how her words will be heard by Roberta, as well as how Roberta might respond. Your script should incorporate the rationalizations or responses that you anticipate Roberta voicing and how Dr. Delgado can reply to them. As such, the "script" should be more like a decision-tree than a monologue.

- Remember that the ethical question in this case is not simply what Dr. Delgado would do for herself, but how well she can act on her own values in light of her patient's goals and Roberta's ability to act on them successfully.
- Refer to the rubric and be sure to include all elements listed when creating your script and in preparing for your explanation for why you came up with your script and action strategy.

Case presentation

Roberta, a 23-year-old HIV positive woman, presented to the Emergency Department complaining of cramping abdominal pain for several hours. On physical examination, she was found to be in labor and soon delivered a seemingly healthy baby boy, whom she named Thomas. She stated that she did not know she was pregnant and therefore did not receive prenatal care or HIV medications during her pregnancy or childbirth. Her viral load had been undetectable one year ago and she was told she did not need medications at that time, but she had not been back to see a doctor since then.

Mothers can transmit HIV to their children during pregnancy or childbirth, as well as through their breast milk when breastfeeding. Pregnant women who take HIV medications during pregnancy and delivery can reduce the chances of transmitting the virus to their infants. Most HIV medicines are safe to use during pregnancy, and they don't increase the risk of birth defects. Taking HIV medications during pregnancy can reduce the risk of transmitting the virus to one's infant to less than 5%. In the absence of any intervention during pregnancy or delivery, transmission rates range from 15% to 45%. HIV can be transmitted during breast feeding, with transmission rates between 4% and 22%. Therefore, in the United States, all HIV positive mothers are advised to feed their newborns formula.

Roberta is clearly excited about the birth and appears to be very loving – she is constantly holding the baby and kissing him on the cheek every chance that she gets. Soon after delivery, she asks when she can start breast-feeding. Her physician, Dr. Delgado, tells her that breast feeding is not advisable, to which she replies, "I know that breast milk is good for my baby and my baby deserves the best."

Parents usually serve in the place of children in terms of having the authority to make decisions about their health and determine their course of treatment, based on the presumption that parents will act in the best interests of their children. However, when parents act in ways that may hurt their children, they no longer can serve as substitute decision-makers for them, and it is the physician's fiduciary responsibility to serve his or her patient, in this case, Thomas. Moreover, when parents make decisions that can hurt their children, the courts may intervene to protect them, based on the doctrine of *parens patriae*. Relevant to this situation, in the case of *In Re Tyson*, the court ruled that it is illegal for an HIV positive mother to breastfeed her child.[1] In this case, the court mandated that the parents may maintain physical custody of the child, yet the court awarded the state legal custody and medical decision-making authority on the child's behalf. Court appointed monitors checked the parents' compliance through weekly visits. Also, the New York State Department of Health published its policy statement on situations where breastfeeding is contraindicated or not advisable in 2018, in which it states regarding women living with HIV,

> Numerous organizations recommend that women living with HIV in the United States, where safe infant feeding alternatives are available, should not breastfeed or feed their own expressed breastmilk to their infants. The New York State (NYS) AIDS Institute's Perinatal HIV Prevention Committee clinical guidelines state: "Breastfeeding by HIV-infected women is not recommended, even when the mother is taking combination antiretroviral therapy (ART) and/or her viral load is undetectable. The following factors increase the risk of HIV transmission via breastfeeding: higher levels of HIV RNA in breastmilk; inflammation of the breast (mastitis); longer duration of breastfeeding; or resumption of breastfeeding after abrupt weaning. Although the risk of mother-to-child transmission of HIV is significantly lower with the use of combination ART and an undetectable viral load, neither infant antiretroviral prophylaxis nor suppressive maternal postpartum ART completely eliminates the risk of HIV transmission through breast milk." Therefore, at this time, "Undetectable = Untransmittable (U = U)" does not apply to transmission through breastfeeding.[2]

The legal background presented above supports Dr. Delgado's belief that Roberta should not breastfeed Thomas, but it should not be taken to imply that Dr. Delgado would be at some legal risk if she did not talk to Roberta. Nor does it imply that Dr. Delgado should seek legal intervention, since such escalation might create additional problems without actually solving the issue at hand. The legal background does, however, provide support for Dr. Delgado's decision, in that her desire to act on her values has widespread societal acceptance. She is not alone in her belief that Roberta should not breastfeed.

If Dr. Delgado went to the courts, or even an ethics committee, unnecessarily, Roberta may choose to breastfeed Thomas and not disclose that information to Dr. Delgado or to Thomas's pediatrician. She may even avoid treatment altogether, if she fears that by breastfeeding Thomas, she may face serious consequences. Moreover, based on how Roberta is doting over Thomas, Dr. Delgado knows that she does not intentionally want to hurt her child. Rather, it is more likely that she is unaware of the deleterious effects that breastfeeding may cause Thomas. Dr. Delgado also knows how important loving contact is for a child's development at the beginning of life. As such, she decided to raise her concerns with her again in order to persuade her not to breastfeed Thomas, by informing Roberta of the consequences that breastfeeding may have and by giving her the best treatment protocols for her child. In doing this, Dr. Delgado is recognizing her obligations to the infant and acting in the infant's best interests. She is also giving Roberta the knowledge that she needs to make good healthcare decisions for her child.

Discussion: Who are the key stakeholders and what is at stake for them?

In this situation, the main stakeholders would be Dr. Delgado, Roberta, and Thomas. Dr. Delgado wants to act on her values, but in such a way that Roberta will listen to her. She does not want to inform Roberta in such a way that she either does not get her point across due to technical jargon or because she questions the care that Roberta has for Thomas. Given that she just gave birth to her baby boy, Roberta is in a highly emotional and exhausted state, so she may not be able to fully hear what Dr. Delgado has to say at the time. It is therefore very important to approach the subject in a way that she can understand. Thomas is the primary stakeholder in this case, since there is a risk that Thomas may contract HIV, if he has not already, and may not get proper preventative or therapeutic treatment. If Thomas has already contracted HIV, there may be more benefits to breastfeeding than not, since breastfeeding has nutritional benefits for the baby, as well as medical, psychological, and economic benefits for both mother and child. However, these benefits do not outweigh the risks of transmitting HIV to Thomas. Roberta should therefore not risk infecting Thomas until it can be confirmed whether he has contracted HIV or not.

Even though it is not mentioned in the case presentation, a possible stakeholder may be Thomas's father, who, if he is known, would have certain parental rights and obligations towards Thomas.

Additional stakeholders could be other members of the healthcare team, the hospital, and the court system. If Roberta is not persuaded by Dr. Delgado, the hospital ethics committee may have to get involved on behalf of Thomas, and, if the problem escalates, the court system may have to intervene.

Can you think of any other stakeholders? Can you think of what else might be at stake?

What arguments or rationalizations is Dr. Delgado likely to encounter?

We already saw that Roberta thinks that breast milk is good for her baby and that she thinks that Thomas deserves the best. In this case, Dr. Delgado and Roberta agree on the value of giving Thomas the best. The issue, therefore, seems to be that Roberta does not know what the best for Thomas is. In recognizing that Dr. Delgado and Roberta share the common goal of wanting what is best for Thomas, Dr. Delgado can approach the situation from a perspective of shared aspirations rather than from a judgmental or disciplinary stance.

However, Roberta may also respond to Dr. Delgado that she is unable to purchase baby formula or comply with the regimen of tests and infant care for

Thomas. Even if Roberta does not bring this argument up in their conversation, Dr. Delgado should anticipate this argument since Roberta did not receive any prenatal care.

Can you think of other rationalizations that Roberta may offer?

What strategies can Dr. Delgado use to counter Roberta's arguments and plot a course of action for addressing the situation?

In the process of developing a strategy, Dr. Delgado should consider various factors such as Roberta's level of knowledge and ability to follow recommendations, the communication style she uses, who else she includes in the conversation, the availability of information, the complexity of the situation, and risk.

Audience

Dr. Delgado should be aware of the level of Roberta's health knowledge and the resources at her disposal. These factors will affect not only whether Roberta will be persuaded by Dr. Delgado but also whether she will be able to carry out her recommendations. Dr. Delgado should be aware both of her authority in terms of her medical knowledge but also her inability to compel Roberta to comply without resorting to the courts.

Communication style and location

This is a conversation to have in person and, potentially, with the help of Roberta's nurse or the hospital's lactation consultant. Dr. Delgado (and the other members of the healthcare team that she includes in the conversation) should make it clear that she appreciates the love that Roberta has for Thomas and that she does not question Roberta's desire to give Thomas the best. However, Dr. Delgado should also make it clear that Roberta's decision to breastfeed Thomas is not in line with Roberta's values to give Thomas the best, since it might impose a risk on him. Emphasis should be on the positive side, i.e. that giving formula is a better alternative, rather than on the negative, i.e. that breastfeeding is bad.

In communicating to Roberta, Dr. Delgado can open the conversation by validating Roberta's desire to breastfeed, and by asking her questions with the purpose of trying to understand her motivations to do so. By validating Roberta's desire to breastfeed, even while not endorsing it, Dr. Delgado can begin discussing various options with Roberta from a position where Roberta knows that Dr. Delgado respects her values and concerns. This will allow Roberta to be more open to discussion since she will not feel defensive or ignored. In addition to her awareness of the health benefits of breastfeeding, there may be social or cultural pressure to breastfeed or stigma if Roberta doesn't. The social pressures to breastfeed might also elicit guilt, which Roberta might not know how to deal with. Bringing in a social worker or a psychologist might help Roberta if she needs it.

Availability of information and data

To avoid any of the rationalizations that Roberta may give, Dr. Delgado should be prepared with the information needed to show Roberta why giving Thomas formula or banked breast milk is in his best interests. She should also have information about which formulas to use and how to purchase them. For example, if Roberta qualifies for it, Medicaid covers the cost of infant formula, though each state's Medicaid program has its own criteria regarding coverage of infant formula. Also, some states have laws requiring insurance providers to cover certain types of medical food based on a child's diagnosis. The Special Supplemental Nutrition Program for Women, Infants, and Children (WIC) may also be a resource for Roberta to help her with supplemental foods, health care referrals, and nutrition education.[3] The Human Milk Banking Association of North America (HMBANA) may also be able to help Roberta receive breastmilk for Thomas, even if she cannot afford to pay for it.[4] Dr. Delgado may not have all of the information needed to advise Roberta properly, but she can ask other members of the healthcare team, such as a lactation consultant, social worker, or patient manager to help provide Roberta with the information that she would need.

Another alternative, which is less optimal, is for Roberta to flash heat her expressed breastmilk before bottle-feeding it to Thomas. This would reduce the risk of transmission, and would not compromise the nutritional benefits of the milk.[5] If Roberta cannot obtain formula or banked breastmilk, this could be an option. However, flash heating is time consuming and, if there is social pressure to breastfeed then this may not help Roberta.

Dr. Delgado should also be prepared to discuss how Roberta will comply with getting Thomas the necessary tests and medicine in the first months of his life. She can get this information from the hospital's patient engagement officer, or even bring the officer into the conversation. The engagement officer might also have resources at his or her disposal to help Roberta obtain the formula that Thomas needs.

Complexity of the situation

While the nature of the situation is relatively straightforward in terms of the decision not to have Roberta breastfeed Thomas, Roberta's current state and the socio-economic factors in the case add complexity to the situation in terms of how to communicate and what population-based issues to confront. This demands that Dr. Delgado's strategy balances the tension between persuading Roberta to change her mind and giving her the ability to follow through with Dr. Delgado's health plan for Thomas.

Risks

The most obvious risk is that Roberta either does not listen to Dr. Delgado or is unable to carry out her health plan for Thomas. If handled incorrectly, Thomas will be exposed to avoidable risk of contracting HIV or to not getting the proper treatment, which may lead to potential negative health consequences.

Potential strategy

Once Dr. Delgado considers these factors, she can begin to develop a plan to raise her concerns with Roberta. One potential strategy to apply in this case would be identifying and reaching out to allies and generating alternative approaches to the current challenges. Dr. Delgado can reach out to other members of the health care team who may be better acquainted with Roberta and her socio-economic challenges to ensure that Roberta is able and willing to listen. She should also be equipped with alternative strategies to allow Roberta to act on her own interest of giving Thomas the best. In this way, Dr. Delgado will not only be able to act on her own values but she will be empowering Roberta to act on hers as well.

How can Dr. Delgado address the matter in a conversation with Roberta? What should she say and what support should she, or should she not, utilize? What other information could Dr. Delgado obtain prior to the conversation with Roberta to help her explain the options in a way that validates Roberta's desire to be a good mother to Thomas while encouraging the choice to use formula?

Case 3: Reporting a colleague

Assignment

In this case, you will read about Dr. James Fischer, an orthopedic surgeon, who tells his colleague, Dr. Samuel Fischbein, about his medical condition which may threaten patients' welfare. Dr. Fischbein decides to speak to him about reporting himself to his supervisor or the hospital administration. After reading the case presentation and discussion, prepare an action plan and script for Dr. Fischbein's conversation with Dr. Fischer.

- You are not given Dr. Fischbein's complete personal–professional profile in the case description. Before preparing your action plan and script for Dr. Fischbein, please create a personal–professional profile for him and think about how his personal–professional profile affects the emotional impact the case has on him both positively and negatively. Also, consider how his profile shapes which action strategy would be most effective.
- Your action strategy should include plans for gathering the additional information he might need, recognizing and utilizing any opportunities that may be available, identifying and mitigating any challenges that he might foresee, and crafting alternative solutions that incorporate these factors.
- In preparing your script, consider not only Dr. Fischbein's own perspective, but also the perspectives of Dr. Fischer. Think about the actual words you would have Dr. Fischbein say and how his words will be heard by Dr. Fischer, as well as how Dr. Fischer might respond. Your script should incorporate the rationalizations or responses that you anticipate Dr. Fischer voicing and how

Dr. Fischbein can reply to them. As such, the "script" should be more like a decision-tree than a monologue.
- Remember that the ethical question in this case is not simply what Dr. Fischbein would do for himself, but how well he can act on his own values in light of his and Dr. Fischer's shared goals and their ability to act on them successfully.
- Refer to the rubric and be sure to include all elements listed when creating your script and in preparing for your explanation for why you came up with your script and action strategy.

Case presentation

Dr. James Fischer, an orthopedic surgeon, comes to Dr. Samuel Fischbein, a psychiatrist, for an evaluation. James and Samuel have been friends since medical school, where James introduced Samuel to his wife. Samuel knows that James has a history of seizures since childhood and has been on anti-epileptic medications since then. He had been seizure-free for many years, but he recently had a complex partial seizure at home, which was witnessed by his wife. The seizure lasted only 30 seconds, and, since his wife is a physician as well, they did not seek additional care at the time. Even though Samuel is not a neurologist, James trusts him and came to him as a friend as much as he came to him as a patient.

He tells Samuel that this was the first time he had experienced a seizure in a long time. He knows he needs to see his neurologist, but his neurologist is away for two weeks and James has a very busy operating scheduling coming up. He wants to make sure he does not have any more seizures in the near future, so he asks Samuel to prescribe him an additional anti-epileptic medication to tide him over until he can get in to see his neurologist. He adds that until the medicine starts to take effect, he plans to have his wife drive him to work. Samuel knows, however, that even after the medicine takes effect, James will not be able perform surgery (or even drive) for a while if ever again. Whether or not James will be able to do so depends on the extent of his condition, the efficacy of the medication, and not having a seizure for a certain period of time determined by state laws and hospital policies. Samuel and James work at the same hospital, and Samuel knows that the incident must be reported to James's supervisor or the hospital administration. Ideally, James should report the incident himself, but, if he refuses to do so, Samuel knows that he must report him.

Discussion: Who are the key stakeholders and what is at stake for them?

The key stakeholders in this case are Dr. Samuel Fischbein, Dr. James Fischer, Dr. Fischer's patients, and the hospital where Dr. Fischer performs surgery. If James were to have a seizure during surgery, he can seriously hurt one of his patients. Moreover, if James knows that he might have a seizure and does not refrain from doing surgery, he risks being sued for malpractice and medical negligence. The hospital may also be included in the lawsuit. Even though he came to Samuel as a patient, and Samuel would have a general obligation to maintain patient confidentiality, patient confidentiality is deferred out of a duty to report when there is a good chance that the patient can hurt other people. Depending on how Samuel confronts James, he may risk losing a friendship that he values.

Can you think of any other stakeholders? Can you think of what else might be at stake?

What arguments or rationalizations is Samuel likely to encounter?

James might argue that he had only one incident and that by taking additional anti-epileptic medication he will not have any more seizures. He could tell Samuel that he will make sure to add more checks and support to his team that will mitigate any risk of harm if he ever has a seizure again. James may also play on Samuel's loyalty to him as a friend, by trying to persuade Sam to allow him to deal with his condition without involving anyone else. He may say that by reporting him, when he can control his seizures, Samuel would cause him to lose his job unnecessarily. James may also tell Sam that he will tell his supervisor, yet not actually do so.

Can you think of other rationalizations that James may offer?

What strategies can Samuel use to counter James's arguments and plot a course of action for addressing the situation?

In the process of developing a strategy, Samuel should consider various factors such as what is at stake for the different stakeholders, the communication style he uses, the availability of hospital policies that cover these types of situations, and the complexity of the situation.

Audience and communication style

James is both Samuel's friend and a colleague at the hospital, so Samuel would be personally aware of what is at stake for James in this situation, in terms of the personal risks of losing his livelihood and the professional risks of harming his patients. Also, if Samuel were simply to tell James that he has a duty to report him, Samuel would be putting a strain on both his personal and professional relationship with James by putting James on the defensive and potentially making him regret coming to Samuel for help in the first place.

As such, Samuel should try to speak with James in a way that persuades him to report himself and follow the proper procedures in a way that does not threaten their relationship. Sam should also make sure that James knows that Sam will hold James accountable for reporting the incident, since it not only affects his future patients but it affects both James's and Samuel's professional integrity.

Samuel could put his position in writing, so that James could have time to reflect on Samuel's position and understand the ramifications of the situation. Yet, by putting his position in writing, it may also seem that Samuel is trying to protect his own professional position. Moreover, by writing to James before speaking to him, Samuel may be escalating the situation before giving James time to speak to his supervisor.

Availability of hospital policies

When speaking to James, Samuel should have James consider the hospital policies regarding reporting other physician's conduct as well as policies regarding the hospital's responsibilities to impaired physicians. While each hospital will have its own policies, each hospital will most likely have policies that put into practice the guidelines of the American Medical Association Code of Medical Ethics. For example, the Code's Opinion 9.4.2 states that when physicians become aware of conduct that threatens patient welfare, they should do the following, starting with the first step and continuing to the other steps if the conduct continues:

a Report the conduct to appropriate clinical authorities in the first instance so that the possible impact on patient welfare can be assessed and remedial action taken. This should include notifying the peer review body of the hospital, or the local or state medical society when the physician of concern does not have hospital privileges.
b Report directly to the state licensing board when the conduct in question poses an immediate threat to the health and safety of patients or violates state licensing provisions.
c Report to a higher authority if the conduct continues unchanged despite initial reporting.
d Protect the privacy of any patients who may be involved to the greatest extent possible, consistent with due process.
e Report the suspected violation to appropriate authorities.[6]

However, reporting should not be seen as punitive, but rather as a means to provide support and care for one's colleague. The AMA's Code of Medical Ethics, Opinion 9.3.2, states that even when reporting physicians with physical or mental health conditions that interfere with their ability and can put patients at risk, impaired physicians are deserving of thoughtful, compassionate care, which includes ensuring that impaired colleagues receive appropriate assistance from a physician health program to recover as well as professional assistance when they resume patient care.[7]

Complexity of the situation

While the nature of the situation is relatively straightforward in terms of the obligation to report the incident, the relationship between James and Samuel add complexity to the situation in terms of how Samuel should communicate with James about the issue. This demands that Samuel's strategy balances the tension between persuading James to report himself and making sure that, if he does not do so, James is aware that Samuel will report him.

Potential strategy

Once Samuel considers these factors, he can begin to develop a plan to raise his concerns with James. One potential strategy to apply in this case would be bridging the gap, by making a connection between their shared professional mission and the actions he proposes. Samuel should try to offer that prescribing James anti-epileptics is not a sufficient course of action in this case because he wouldn't be able to return to surgery immediately after starting medication and that James needs to think about his professional responsibilities to his patients.

In addition, because James will not be able to perform surgery for an extended period of time, if ever again, Sam could help James generate alternative approaches to the current challenges and reframe the issue, by having James think about how he can serve in different medical capacities if he can no longer do surgery because of a risk of seizures. It would be helpful to have James consider what other roles he currently plays on the health care team and what else he may see himself doing in the future.

If James does not want to listen and simply wants Samuel to prescribe medication so that he can return to work, Samuel could respond by saying that treating seizure patients is not within the scope of his practice and he would not feel comfortable prescribing and managing his medications. Samuel could then let James know that he will have to go to someone else, who might report him in a way that is more detrimental than if James reports himself.

An important aspect to consider is when Samuel should discuss the issue with James. Samuel could raise his concerns with James when James first comes to see him, yet Samuel may not be aware of all the policies and procedures that he could use to persuade James to report himself. Alternatively, James may not be ready to hear about what his recent seizure means for his future practice, and he may need time to come to terms with this big change in his professional life. In thinking about how to respond to James's request, Samuel can think about his action plan as a process. He can first talk to James about his seizure as a friend to see how it has affected James in general. After discussing the experience, they could set up a time in the near future to discuss how to proceed moving forward. In the meantime, Samuel could seek the support he may need to be persuasive. The ability to take time in raising his concerns, however, depends on how time-sensitive the issue is. Does James have a full patient load, and therefore, is immediate action necessary? Or has James already realized that he may need to take some time before returning to work?

How can Samuel address the matter in a conversation with James? What should he say and what support should he or should he not utilize?

Case 4: Talking to family members about a patient's medical information

Assignment

In this case, you will read about Dr. Smith, an inpatient physician who is taking care of Mrs. Henderson, and how Mrs. Henderson's children request that they receive information about their mother's condition instead of her. Dr. Smith decides to tell them that he cannot honor that request. After reading the case presentation and discussion, prepare an action plan and script for Dr. Smith's conversation with Mrs. Henderson's children.

- You are not given Dr. Smith's complete personal–professional profile in the case description. Before preparing your action plan and script for Dr. Smith, please create a personal–professional profile for him and think about how his personal–professional profile affects the emotional impact the case has on him both positively and negatively. Also, consider how his profile shapes which action strategy would be most effective.
- Your action strategy should include plans for gathering the additional information he might need, identifying and approaching allies who may be helpful (including which other medical professionals might be helpful to include in your strategy, what their roles might be, and what resources they may have which can help implement your plan successfully), recognizing and utilizing any opportunities that may be available, identifying and mitigating any challenges that he might foresee, and crafting alternative solutions that incorporate these factors.
- In preparing your script, consider not only Dr. Smith's own perspective, but also the perspectives of Mrs. Henderson and her children. What emotions might Mrs. Henderson and her children be having at this time? Think about the actual words you would have Dr. Smith say and how his words will be heard by Mrs. Henderson's children, as well as how they might respond. Your script should incorporate the rationalizations or responses that you anticipate Mrs. Henderson's children voicing and how Dr. Smith can reply to them. As such, the "script" should be more like a decision-tree than a monologue.
- Remember that the ethical question in this case is not simply what Dr. Smith would do for himself, but how well he can act on his own values in light of his, Mrs. Henderson's, and her children's shared goals.
- Refer to the rubric and be sure to include all elements listed when creating your script and in preparing for your explanation for why you came up with your script and action strategy.

Case presentation

Dr. Smith is the inpatient physician taking care of Mrs. Henderson, an elderly woman who will likely be diagnosed with metastatic cancer pending the results of a biopsy. She had been living independently in her home and was brought into the hospital by her daughter, who lives down the street from her, several days ago because her daughter noticed that she wasn't eating and she was staying in bed more often. Mrs. Henderson said that she had been having abdominal pains for the past month and lost her appetite, and has lost about ten pounds. Her abdominal CT scan showed a large mass in one of her ovaries, as well as lesions in her liver and lungs.

Mrs. Henderson is alert and talkative to the medical staff, she had a cognitive assessment and was determined to have capacity. Nevertheless, she is very sick, and her children have concerns about how she may react to the test results. They also fear that there might not be any cure for what she might have, and they worry that any conversation the medical team has with her might cause her to become despondent. They want to protect her from any unnecessary bad news, so they ask Dr. Smith to inform them first about the results of the biopsy. Dr. Smith knows that he has an obligation to tell Mrs. Henderson and that he cannot give the test results to her family without Mrs. Henderson's explicit consent.

Discussion: Who are the key stakeholders and what is at stake for them?

In this situation, the main stakeholders would be Dr. Smith, Mrs. Henderson, and her family. Dr. Smith knows that the obligation to inform patients directly of any medical tests and to communicate with them directly about treatment plans is based on three ethical and professional principles, namely: (1) the right to one's medical information, (2) the value of patient autonomy, and (3) one's fiduciary responsibility to one's patient. Even though many states do not have clear legislation as to who owns the information in a physician's medical records, many states do have laws that give patients the right to access their medical records, regardless of ownership status. Also, patients have the right to access their medical records under the HIPAA Privacy and Security Rules. Withholding information from patients does not respect their rights to their medical information.

Moreover, the patient has a right to self-determination, as part of the principle of autonomy, which means that the physician has a responsibility to enable the patient to make autonomous decisions. Since there will be additional decisions to make with regards to how treatment or palliative care should proceed, the patient needs to be informed of her diagnosis and prognosis. While there is a medical ethics concept called therapeutic privilege, which is an exception to the duty to inform patients of their diagnosis, this exception only applies when disclosing information would pose a serious psychological threat to the patient. The proper exercise of therapeutic privilege has a high bar and this case does not warrant it. Cases where therapeutic privilege is invoked typically involve situations where there is a grave risk to the patient's safety or a question regarding the patient's capacity. In this case, the patient clearly has capacity and there is no reason to presume that the diagnostic information in and of itself will cause a shock or a psychological threat.

Thirdly, a physician's fiduciary obligation is to act in the best interests of his or her patient, which should not be overridden by requests of the patient's family members. While family members sometimes can – and do – make health care decisions on behalf of patients, this is only justified when family members serve as substitute decision makers in situations where the patient lacks capacity or when the family member is explicitly given durable power of attorney (durable power of attorney can transfer responsibilities to an agent immediately or it can go into effect when the patient loses capacity, depending on how it is written). In this case, the patient is competent, so there is no need for substituted judgment by a proxy. Nor is there any mention that the patient specifically gave a family member power of attorney.

By asking the physician not to disclose the information to the patient, the family members are asking not only the physician, but the whole collaborative care team, to dismiss their professional values and to engage in deception. Moreover, because the patient is alert, she might already suspect a diagnosis or will find out at some point in the future. Therefore, maintaining such deception will hurt the patient–physician relationship. The family is not malicious in requesting to hear the information first. They are just seeing the situation, given their own biases and values, without considering what is at stake and the ramifications for the medical team or their mother, Mrs. Henderson.

While it does not seem to be the case with Mrs. Henderson's family, when faced with end-of-life care and palliative care decisions, there may be times when a relative might have a vested interest, whether to prolong a patient's life out of his or her own desires and not in fulfillment of the patient's wishes or even to expedite death if he or she is a beneficiary in the will. In these situations, physicians need to affirm the best interests of the patient and make sure that they can engage in clear communication with the patient, whether separately or with family members present.

Can you think of any other stakeholders? Can you think of what else might be at stake?

What arguments or rationalizations is Dr. Smith likely to encounter?

Mrs. Henderson's children are likely to justify their request to be informed first by saying that it would be best for their mother. They might argue that their mother will not be able to handle the information and the results could make her condition worse. They might also say that since they will be taking care of her, they have a right to know, or that the rest of the family will want to help her in her time of need. They may dismiss hospital policies and medical ethics principles that affirm patient confidentiality and that preclude them from being informed without their mother's consent by saying that they are simply meant to protect the medical team and the hospital from a lawsuit, but they are not in the best interests of their mother.

Can you think of other rationalizations that the family may offer?

What strategies can Dr. Smith use to counter the family's arguments and plot a course of action for addressing the situation?

Even though Dr. Smith knows that the proper response to the family is to tell them that he is obligated to inform the patient of his findings, he should not simply dismiss the family's concerns. The family members' concerns are grounded in their experience with, and care for, their mother. Also, the family will be the ones to oversee Mrs. Henderson's care when she returns home. As such, treatment alternatives might need to incorporate their cooperation. Also, there may be cultural factors that are in play. For example, certain cultures are less individualistic and it is the norm for certain family members to make decisions for others. If this is the case, the patient may not want to know her medical information. One potential strategy to apply in this case would be to listen actively to the family's request and, on hearing their concerns, clarify their misconceptions and incorporate their concerns.

When responding to the family members, certain points may help make his strategy more effective: When speaking to the family members, Dr. Smith can show empathy for their situation and reassure them that he has the patient's best interests in mind. When telling them about his ethical and legal obligations, he can also let them know that he will not force information on their mother. Rather, he will ask her if she wants the test results explained to her alone, with a family member present, or if she would prefer that he speak directly with a family member. If Mrs. Henderson decides to include her children in hearing about the results, then he will of course include them in whatever way Mrs. Henderson requests. Dr. Smith can also reassure the family by telling them that he can imagine the distress the medical information may cause, and that he will make sure to speak to their mother slowly and clearly, using plain language and not jargon, and that he will discuss different options and alternatives in addition to providing the test results so that she is not left with a feeling that there is nothing left to do. Through empathetic listening, Dr. Smith can also show Mrs. Henderson's children that they are not being ignored and that they are all working together to care for their mother.

It may be the case that the children are also in need of a professional with whom to speak regarding their own feelings and emotions, as well as how to care for their mother, given her deteriorating health. Those conversations may be better suited for a different member of the collaborative care team, such as a chaplain or social worker.

How can Dr. Smith address the matter in a conversation with Mrs. Henderson's children? What should he say and what support should he, or should he not, utilize?

Case 5: Speaking to a colleague about a patient's complaints

Assignment

In this case, you will read about Dr. Melinda Bateman, who hears complaints about Dr. Steve Goldfarb from his patient Johan, when she was covering for him while he was on vacation. Dr. Bateman decides to confront Dr. Goldfarb about what the patient said. After reading the case presentation and discussion, prepare an action plan and script for Dr. Bateman's conversation with Dr. Goldfarb.

- You are not given Dr. Bateman's complete personal–professional profile in the case description. Before preparing your action plan and script for Dr. Bateman, please create a personal–professional profile for her and think about how her personal–professional profile affects the emotional impact the case has on her both positively and negatively. Also, consider how her profile shapes which action strategy would be most effective.
- Your action strategy should include plans for gathering the additional information she might need, identifying and approaching allies who may be helpful (including which other medical professionals might be helpful to include in your strategy, what their roles might be, and what resources they may have which can help implement your plan successfully), recognizing and utilizing any opportunities that may be available, identifying and mitigating any challenges that she might foresee, and crafting alternative solutions that incorporate these factors.
- In preparing your script, consider not only Dr. Bateman's own perspective, but also the perspectives of Dr. Goldfarb and Johan. Think about the actual words you would have Dr. Bateman say and how her words will be heard by Dr. Goldfarb, as well as how he might respond. Your script should incorporate the rationalizations or responses that you anticipate Dr. Goldfarb voicing and how Dr. Bateman can reply to them. As such, the "script" should be more like a decision-tree than a monologue.
- Remember that the ethical question in this case is not simply what Dr. Bateman would do for herself, but how well she can act on her own values in light of her and Dr. Goldfarb's shared goals.
- Refer to the rubric and be sure to include all elements listed when creating your script and in preparing for your explanation for why you came up with your script and action strategy.

Case presentation

Dr. Steve Goldfarb works in a practice with Dr. Melinda Bateman, and he asked Melinda to cover for him while he goes on vacation with his family. While away, Johan Sternbuch, one of Steve's patients, comes in to the office complaining about lower back pain. Melinda looks at Johan's chart and sees that he has had x-rays, an MRI, and has taken a number of different opioids for pain management. When asked about therapeutic treatments and medications, Johan says he hasn't tried physical therapy or regular acetaminophen with non-steroidal analgesics but would be open to trying them. As Melinda begins to ask him more questions about his pain, Johan starts to tell her how he doesn't think that Dr. Goldfarb is taking his pain seriously and questions whether Dr. Goldfarb is a qualified physician or simply a drug dealer. He explains that his consultations are always very short: Dr. Goldfarb seems disinterested in listening to him describe the pain, and quickly writes him a script for opioids usually without even examining his back. He says he is feeling so frustrated that Dr. Goldfarb is not caring for him properly that he is thinking about making a complaint. Melinda sees that Johan is in pain and that he feels like he has no one with whom to discuss his concerns, yet Melinda also does not want to criticize Dr. Goldfarb in front of his patient. She has never heard other complaints about her colleague, but she also has never really had the opportunity to hear anything about Dr. Goldfarb's practice either. She is concerned and decides to raise her concerns with her colleague when he returns, but at the moment advises Johan to bring up his concerns with Dr. Goldfarb as well. She tells him that it is important to make sure that his doctor knows how he feels to see if the relationship can change before filing a complaint or switching doctors. Dr. Bateman does not need to ask Johan's permission to raise her concerns with Dr. Goldfarb, since both she and Dr. Goldfarb have a patient–physician relationship with Johan and are therefore permitted to consult with each other about Johan's care. Nevertheless, she may want to tell Johan that she will be updating Dr. Goldfarb about the visit to make sure that Johan's treatment plan best suits Johan's goals for pain management. This would allow Johan to feel as if he is being heard without committing Dr. Bateman to take a particular stance without first getting more information. If he says that he does not want her to speak to Dr. Goldfarb, however, then Dr. Bateman should explain to Johan that her discussion with Dr. Goldfarb will center on Johan's desired course of pain management, and re-emphasize the importance of Johan bringing up his personal concerns with Dr. Goldfarb.

In deciding to raise her concerns with Dr. Goldfarb, Dr. Bateman would need to think about who the various stakeholders are and what was at stake for them, as well as how she could raise her concern and still maintain a stable working relationship with her colleague.

Discussion: Who are the key stakeholders and what is at stake for them?

The key stakeholders in this case are Dr. Melinda Bateman, Dr. Steve Goldfarb, and Johan Sternbuch. Once Dr. Bateman sees Johan as a patient, they initiate a patient–physician relationship whereby she has a fiduciary responsibility to him. She thereby has an interest in Johan's health and making sure that he receives the best care possible. The way in which she approaches Johan's concerns should demonstrate empathy; she should show that she is listening to Johan and that she appreciates how his experience with Dr. Goldfarb is affecting him. Yet, Dr. Bateman does not know the history and context of Dr. Goldfarb's relationship with Johan or whether this is a unique case or one example that could be found among many. Dr. Bateman must be careful not to openly criticize Dr. Goldfarb without knowing more information, even when she tells Johan that his feelings and experience are legitimate. If she were to openly criticize Dr. Goldfarb, she runs the risk of incorrectly castigating him and potentially escalating the situation unnecessarily.

If Johan's experience reveals a broader perception held by Dr. Goldfarb's patients, however, then Dr. Goldfarb might be putting his other patients and the medical practice as a whole at risk. Dr. Goldfarb's other patients may not be sharing necessary information with Dr. Goldfarb or may be harmed due to Dr. Goldfarb's potential inattentiveness. As Drs. Bateman and Goldfarb are members of a general partnership, if Dr. Goldfarb is sued for malpractice, Dr. Bateman can also have the suit brought against her as well.

Can you think of any other stakeholders? Can you think of what else might be at stake?

What arguments or rationalizations is Dr. Bateman likely to encounter?

When Dr. Bateman raises her concerns to Dr. Goldfarb, he may minimize Johan's credibility or the degree to which Johan's concerns should be taken seriously. He can say that Johan's complaints are based on the fact that Johan was upset that he was not given the prescription that he wanted on his last visit. He may even say that the last time Johan came to visit, he did, in fact, have less time to see him than usual, but there were a lot of unexpected visits from patients that day which normally does not happen.

Dr. Goldfarb might also say that Dr. Bateman is not responsible for policing the other doctors in the practice and that she should focus on her own patients. This rationalization attempts to shift the locus of responsibility away from Dr. Bateman, by saying, in essence, it is not her problem. This rationalization is oftentimes used to prevent a person from taking action. In this case in particular, however, it should be seen as ineffective, since Johan has become Dr. Bateman's problem by becoming her patient.

Can you think of other rationalizations that Dr. Goldfarb may offer?

What strategies can Dr. Bateman use to counter Dr. Goldfarb's arguments and plot a course of action for addressing the situation?

In the process of developing a strategy, Dr. Bateman should consider various factors, such as the accuracy and prevalence of her concerns, the communication style and the location where she decides to raise her concerns, the availability of information and data, the complexity of the situation, and risk.

Audience

Dr. Bateman should be aware of her current relationship with Dr. Goldfarb and how he might take her concerns. She should recognize that she has much less experience with Johan (and Dr. Goldfarb's other patients) than he does; she should, therefore, pose her concerns in a way that shows respect to her colleague. Dr. Bateman could also consider if there is anyone else with whom she might want to speak before talking to Dr. Goldfarb. For example, she could talk with the nurses who work with Dr. Goldfarb to treat Johan to see if they have encountered anything that could shed light on Johan's complaint. While this option might have the benefit of getting more insight into Johan as a patient, it may look like Dr. Bateman is questioning Dr. Goldfarb's patient care. If she were to ask other colleagues about Johan, she must make sure not to do so in a way that might be perceived as a slight against Dr. Goldfarb.

What advantages and disadvantages might there be in approaching others before talking with Dr. Goldfarb?

Communication style

Dr. Bateman's communication style should make it clear that she respects Dr. Goldfarb as a colleague and is not questioning his integrity or, in general, his patient care. She should make clear, however, that Johan's concerns are valid and may reflect a general perception of Dr. Goldfarb's patient management. If Johan's perception is accurate and generally held, then Dr. Goldfarb may not be giving his patients the time and attention needed for good medical care. If they are not, they still reflect a need for better communication between Dr. Goldfarb and Johan.

Because Dr. Goldfarb is away on vacation, Dr. Bateman could either reach out to him while he is away or wait until he returns. The timing of her communication and whether it is in person, on the phone, or in an email, could impact whether Dr. Goldfarb is inclined to hear her concerns or not. Moreover, the formality of writing one's concerns might put Dr. Goldfarb on the defensive.

Availability of information and data

Because Dr. Bateman and Dr. Goldfarb work in the same practice, to avoid any of the rationalizations that Dr. Goldfarb may give, Dr. Bateman should be prepared to ask Dr. Goldfarb to consider his care of patients by looking at the information in their medical charts and on hearing the perspectives from the nurses and other medical staff that work with him. Dr. Bateman should point to these resources as ways for Dr. Goldfarb to consider his own quality of care rather than be seen as a means to investigate him. If Dr. Bateman would look at Dr. Goldfarb's records for patients with whom she does not have a patient–physician relationship it may be a breach of patient confidentiality. Yet, even if she does have a legal relationship with patients, if she were to look at patient data without first talking to Dr. Goldfarb, it may be seen by Dr. Goldfarb as a breach of loyalty and trust between colleagues.

Complexity of the situation

This situation is actually quite complex since Dr. Bateman has relatively little information at present and the manner in which she seeks to obtain more information might negatively impact her efficacy in voicing her concerns about what

Johan told her about Dr. Goldfarb. Moreover, if her concerns are warranted, the consequences of bringing her concerns to Dr. Goldfarb will impact how the practice will handle his level of patient care. If her concerns are not warranted, the consequences might negatively impact their professional relationship without good reason. This demands that Dr. Bateman's strategy balances the tension between respecting Dr. Goldfarb's practice and respecting her obligations to Johan to ensure that he receives proper care.

Risks

The most obvious risk is that speaking up may negatively impact the working relationship between Dr. Bateman and Dr. Goldfarb. If handled incorrectly, it will be very difficult for them to continue to work together. It may also hinder improvement in care for Dr. Goldfarb's patients. If Johan's complaint reveals a more pervasive issue and Dr. Bateman does not speak to Dr. Goldfarb, she may be putting the quality of patient care, as well as the practice's reputation, at risk.

Potential strategy

Once Dr. Bateman considers these factors, she can begin to develop a plan to raise her concerns with Dr. Goldfarb. One potential strategy to apply in this case would be to tell Dr. Goldfarb of her experience in seeing Johan and Johan's current goals for care as a way first to gather more information on Dr. Goldfarb's professional relationship with Johan and then to introduce her concerns if warranted. In this way, she is following up on her patient with his primary physician so that there is continuity of care. Once Dr. Bateman and Dr. Goldfarb are discussing Johan's health and health goals, Dr. Goldfarb may be more open and willing to discuss how Johan's previous treatment plan does not fit with his current expectations for treatment. This would allow Dr. Bateman to see that Johan gets the type of care he wants without challenging Dr. Goldfarb's previous interactions directly.

Another potential strategy to apply would be mental imagery. Through the tool of mental imagery, Dr. Bateman would tell Dr. Goldfarb of Johan's concerns and ask him to imagine how he would have responded to Johan if he were there instead of her. How would he have felt if he heard a patient question his level of care? How would he have listened to Johan and responded to his concerns? In hearing what Johan said, how could he reflect on his own standard of care to think about how he could improve? Instead of simply asking Dr. Goldfarb to think about the answers to these questions, Dr. Bateman can let him know that Johan will in fact bring up his concerns at his next visit and can offer to role play so that Dr. Goldfarb can be prepared for when he comes. By using this strategy, Dr. Bateman can get more information about the credibility of Johan's concerns and learn whether they reflect a broader concern for Dr. Goldfarb's patients, without having to challenge him. Rather than be oppositional, she can work collaboratively with Dr. Goldfarb to consider how to move forward. By exposing his biases through mental imagery and role play, Dr. Bateman can help Dr. Goldfarb appreciate what his behavior and communication conveys to his patients about his attention and care for them, so that he can be intrinsically motivated to change his habits. In this way, Dr. Bateman is not challenging her colleague directly, but rather is looking for ways to give voice to her concerns in a way that also helps her colleague give voice to his own professional values.

It may be the case, however, that Dr. Goldfarb is unwilling to listen to Dr. Bateman about her concerns, regardless of how Dr. Bateman approaches him about them. He may be aware of his lack of quality of care for patients and simply not care. However, Dr. Bateman has no reason to assume this at the outset and should try to give voice to her values in a way that gives Dr. Goldfarb the benefit of the doubt until shown incorrect.

How can Dr. Bateman bring up her conversation with Johan to Dr. Goldfarb? What should she say and what support should she, or should she not, utilize?

Case 6: Complementary and alternative medicine

Assignment

In this case, you will read about Ms. P., a colleague's patient, who decides to pursue alternative medicine rather than take your colleague's medical recommendations. Ms. P.'s husband does not support her decision. Your colleague asks you how you would handle the situation and whether she should no longer see Ms. P. as a patient. After reading the case presentation and discussion, prepare a script for your conversation with your colleague.

- Decisions to consider are whether your colleague should stop seeing Ms. P. as a patient or continue the patient–physician relationship and, if to continue, how to inform Ms. P. of the risks of relying (solely) on alternative medicine for her treatment plan.
- Please use your own personal–professional profile (or one on which your small group agrees for the purpose of this exercise) and think about how your personal–professional profile affects how you decide to counsel your colleague in responding to Ms. P. as well as how your profile shapes the way in which you communicate that decision.
- Your action strategy should include plans for gathering the additional information you or your colleague might need, identifying and approaching allies who may be helpful, recognizing and utilizing any opportunities that may be available, identifying and mitigating any challenges that you might foresee, and crafting alternative solutions that incorporate these factors.
- In preparing your script, consider not only your own perspective, but also the perspectives of your colleague and Ms. P. How will your colleague take your suggestions? How will Ms. P. react? Think about the actual words you would say and would have your colleague say and how her words will be heard by Ms. P. Your script should incorporate the rationalizations or responses that

you anticipate from your colleague and Ms. P. and how you can reply to them. As such, the "script" should be more like a decision-tree than a monologue.

- Remember that the ethical question in this case is not simply what you would do yourself, but how well your colleague can act on her own values in light of her patient's goals and her patient's ability to act on them successfully.
- Refer to the rubric and be sure to include all elements listed when creating your script and in preparing for your explanation for why you came up with your script and action strategy.

Case presentation

Ms. P., an otherwise healthy 28-year-old woman, sees a naturopath for her primary care.[8] However, Ms. P. is planning to have a child with her husband, who asked if they could make an appointment with a gynecologist since he is worried that she might be getting bad "family-planning" advice. As part of her appointment, the gynecologist performed a Pap smear, in accordance with U.S. Preventive Services Task Force guidelines. The Pap smear revealed low grade squamous intraepithelial neoplasia.[9] Given the Pap smear findings the gynecologist recommended a colposcopy, to which Ms. P. reluctantly agreed. The colposcopy revealed cervical intraepithelial neoplasia 2,[10] a premalignant condition that could progress to invasive adenocarcinoma. The gynecologist then recommended a cervical conization for treatment.[11] Ms. P. told the physician that she plans to follow-up with her naturopath and to pursue meditation, colonics, and yoga, and to work with her Reiki master, trained to perform a type of energy healing that is said to involve moving energy through the body in order to balance it rather than have surgery. She further states that she heard that the conization can make it harder for her to carry a pregnancy to term, and that is a priority for her. She also says that her husband does not support her decision.

Ms. P. and her husband were high school sweethearts and have been married for three years. She graduated college with a Bachelor of Arts and currently works as a preschool teacher. Her husband is a fireman, and the two of them live in a townhouse. Ms. P. does not drink alcohol and has never smoked cigarettes or marijuana. She does yoga or Pilates daily and is a vegetarian. She did not get the human papilloma virus (HPV) vaccine when it was previously offered to her because she heard it had bad side effects.

The gynecologist wants to terminate the patient–physician relationship, but isn't sure if she can. The gynecologist decides to discuss the case with you, and asks you what you would do.

Background to the case

In order to carry out this assignment, you may need some background regarding professional concepts and values to incorporate in your decision-making with respect to this case, in addition to the background we have already learned regarding the patient–physician relationship more generally. From the perspective of professional integrity, it is important to understand the priority of scientific investigation as part of clinical practice. This priority incorporates the notion of evidence-based medicine, the pathophysiological approach to diagnosis and treatment, and clinical experience. From the perspective of patient autonomy, it is important to understand the concepts of informed consent and the right to refuse treatment. From the perspective of the patient–physician relationship, it is important to understand the concept of abandonment.

Evidence-based medicine is an approach to medical decision-making that emphasizes the use of current systematic research in determining the best approach to individual patient care. Evidence-based medicine has been contrasted with other approaches to determining clinical care, most often the pathophysiological approach and clinical experience.

When applied to clinical care, evidence-based decision-making has been broken down into a number of steps, including: (1) turning the information you are seeking into an answerable question, (2) finding the best evidence to answer the question, (3) appraising the evidence in terms of its validity (internal validity),[12] impact,[13] and applicability to the case at hand (external validity),[14] (4) incorporating the answer along with the evidence into a clinical discussion with your patient to arrive at a proper treatment alternative, and (5) evaluating the efficacy of the answer when applied to the treatment of your patient. When used to devise best practices or standards, the steps are very similar, except that environmental assumptions are made for population groups, which may or may not be correct when applied to individuals.

The pathophysiological approach entails the study of pathology, which is the medical discipline that describes what symptoms are observed during disease, with physiology, which is a biological discipline that describes which processes or mechanisms operate in an organism. Together, the two fields endeavor to explain the physiological processes or mechanisms that occur when a person is affected by a disease and how those mechanisms or processes are utilized during treatment.

Clinical experience entails the use of a clinician's familiarity with previous patients' diagnoses and successful treatments as a background to approach new patients and to rely on similar cases previously encountered to set a frame to treat current and future cases.

Proper clinical care, however, must incorporate all three approaches, both for the purpose of understanding diagnoses and effective treatment alternatives, as well as to arrive at treatment decisions that account for an individual patient's condition and values.

From the perspective of understanding diagnoses and effective treatment alternatives, evidence-based medicine and the pathophysiological approach serve to complement each other. For example, given the complexity of the human body, a person may think that he or she understands the pathophysiological mechanisms that are affected by disease and how they operate when a person undergoes a given treatment, yet his or her understanding may not be correct either to predict the success for an individual patient or even for a population. In this instance, clinical research can test pathophysiological understanding to allow for more evidence-based alternatives. On the other hand, clinical research tests whether a particular therapy is successful or not, but it does not explain the processes or mechanisms by which it is successful. This would be the domain of pathophysiology. While the goal for clinical medicine is to treat patients, it is important to learn and to understand about the processes or mechanisms which are affected by disease and which are utilized in treatment to be able to expand the applicability of a research study beyond its original subject population. As such, pathophysiology is critical for the external validity of evidence-based medicine. Moreover, because randomly selected populations are never homogenous, understanding pathophysiological mechanisms can allow physicians to determine whether subject groups are in fact comparable to their individual patients.[15]

Similarly, evidence-based medicine will provide support for which therapies will be most effective in treating a given disease, yet it will not tell a physician which disease a patient has. Recognizing the disease from which a patient may be suffering comes from both understanding pathophysiology and clinical experience.

With respect to applying evidence-based findings to patients, research studies may project which types of treatments may be more effective than others, all things being equal, but in clinical care it is seldom the case that all things are equal. Not only do individual patients have their own values and preferences, but individuals also have different familial, socioeconomic, and other factors which influence the efficacy of a given treatment. When it comes to value premises, evidence-based findings may suggest the most medically or physiologically appropriate treatment, but a patient may value quality of life or home-based therapies over treatments that might allow him or her to live longer but would force the person to visit the doctor or hospital more often. Even for two people who have the same value premises, there might be a difference in efficacy of the same treatment plan, if one person has greater access to care and will not miss doses, while the other does not and might therefore miss doses. These details are significant in determining the best treatment for individual patients, yet they are not factors considered in clinical trials.

While evidence-based medicine has become the principle methodology of physicians for offering medical care, complementary and alternative medicine is still nevertheless popular among many different patient populations. Complementary and alternative medicine (CAM) are those therapies that are believed by their proponents to treat illness or promote health, yet there is not sufficient evidence to support such a claim. For some alternative treatments, there is in fact evidence to support the claim that they either do not promote health or might in fact endanger it. Historically, the medical profession, through the American Medical Association's Code of Ethics, has held a strong stance against using unorthodox therapies.[16] However, today, physicians and other medical providers are more open to incorporating certain complementary and alternative treatments, either because they have been shown to be effective or because patients demand their incorporation. For example, Paul Wolpe writes,

> Over the last thirty years [since the 150th anniversary of the creation of the AMA's Code of Ethics], as alternative medicine has increased its profile, many of the very

> therapies that were being continuously ridiculed by orthodox opponents have been finding their way into the orthodox regime. The importance of nutrition, low-fat diets, and vitamin supplements; the concept of stress as a pathogen; techniques like meditation, yoga, massage, and biofeedback; the use of magnets to cure pain, acupuncture, and a host of pharmaceuticals drawn from traditional medicines – all were once marginalized ideas that were considered by many as quackery.[17]

The decision to include CAM therapies with evidence-based medicine or to endorse CAM therapies when patients ask for them plays off the tension between physician authority and patient autonomy. Issues to consider include: (1) the efficacy or harm of a given therapy (including the placebo effect), (2) endorsement of unscientific therapies and the effect it might have on the view that patients have of the medical profession and EBM, (3) patient autonomy to choose which therapy he or she wants and the incumbent responsibility to be informed of the benefits and detriments of different therapy alternatives, and (4) who will pay for potentially ineffective therapies (whether it be the patient alone or others indirectly through insurance).

Regardless of which treatment path is chosen, before a physician can perform any test or initiate any treatment plan, the patient must give informed consent to the test or treatment. Informed consent entails the following components: (1) capacity/competence, (2) disclosure, (3) understanding, (4) voluntariness, and (5) consent. In this case capacity/competence simply means that the patient has the ability to reason and make her own decisions. Proper disclosure for the purpose of informed consent must include explaining to the patient the risks and benefits of any procedure or treatment in a way that the patient can understand, as well as information on any alternative procedures or treatments from which she can choose. Just as a person has the right to consent to treatment, a person also has the right to refuse treatment. If a physician treats a patient without her consent, it constitutes battery.

Beyond the issues associated with evidence-based medicine and CAM, this case also entails a question about ending the patient–physician relationship. Once such a relationship has been created, physicians cannot suddenly end it, and termination in general is not always so easy. The patient-relationship should last either until both parties agree to end it or when treatment is no longer needed. Because patients are vulnerable, physicians are expected to be more tolerant of patients' nonadherence or other difficulties. When the termination is not handled properly, it is known as abandonment, and it is considered both a form of malpractice, i.e. negligence, and a breach of contract. Abandonment occurs when: (1) care is terminated unilaterally by the physician, (2) the physician does not provide reasonable notice of termination so that the patient cannot find a proper alternative provider, and (3) the patient is still in need of care. Patient abandonment could also occur if physicians were to do the following: (1) fail to transfer a patient to an appropriate level of care, (2) fail to respond to calls from a hospital regarding a patient, (3) refuse to care for a patient after arranging the patient's admission, and (4) fail to treat a patient until new coverage is arranged.[18]

This does not mean that once a relationship exists that a physician must treat a person forever, or as long as the patient wants treatment. There are appropriate reasons for physicians to end the relationship. These include:

1. When there is a breakdown in the relationship that makes it medically impossible to continue treatment.
2. The patient acts in a threatening, abusive, or violent manner, or the patient makes sexual advances to the physician or medical staff.
3. The patient acts in a way that interferes with his or her treatment or safety, including failure to show up at scheduled appointments.
4. The patient refuses to follow the physician's recommended treatment.
5. The patient conceals his or her real identity or engages in fraud or theft.
6. Termination can also be justified for reasons of professional integrity or conscience.

For a physician to end a relationship unilaterally for nondiscriminatory reasons, there are some steps that must be taken to avoid claims of abandonment. Those steps are:

1. Provide the patient with prior notice that his or her behavior will result in the end of the relationship.
2. If the behavior continues, the physician should notify the patient orally and in writing that the relationship will terminate in 30 days or after a time appropriate to find alternative care.
3. The physician should provide the patient with contact information for alternative providers.

Case 7: Talking to patients about assisted reproductive technologies

Assignment

In this case, you will read about a couple who came to your Foundations of Clinical Medicine preceptor's office to talk about pre-implantation genetic diagnosis. Your preceptor asks you how you would advise the couple. After reading the case presentation and discussion, prepare a script for your conversation with your preceptor.

- Decisions to consider are whether your preceptor should talk to the couple about assisted reproductive technology or not, share her own views on the subject or not, and in what to include in her conversation with the couple to help them make an informed decision.
- Please use your own personal–professional profile (or one on which your small group agrees for the purpose of this exercise) and think about how your personal–professional profile affects how you decide to answer your preceptor's

question in how to advise the couple as well as how your profile shapes the way in which you communicate that decision.

- Your action strategy should include plans for gathering the additional information you or your preceptor might need, identifying and approaching allies who may be helpful, recognizing and utilizing any opportunities that may be available, identifying and mitigating any challenges that you might foresee, and crafting alternative solutions that incorporate these factors.
- In preparing your script, consider not only your own perspective, but also the perspectives of your preceptor and the couple. How will your preceptor take your suggestions? How might the couple react to your preceptor's engagement with them? Your script should incorporate the rationalizations or responses that you anticipate from your preceptor and how you can reply to them. As such, the "script" should be more like a decision-tree than a monologue.
- Remember that the ethical question in this case is not simply what you would do yourself, but how well your preceptor can act on her own values in light of her patient's goals and her patient's ability to act on them successfully as well.
- Refer to the rubric and be sure to include all elements listed when creating your script and in preparing for your explanation for why you came up with your script and action strategy.

Case presentation

On Wednesday, when you go to the office of your Foundations of Clinical Medicine preceptor, Dr. Miller, she tells you about a couple that came to see her on the previous Monday. Usually, you simply just shadow your preceptor, she doesn't typically share cases that come up when you are not in her office. She also doesn't engage in a lot of give and take with you when you are in the office; rather, her teaching style is to tell you her thinking process and what she is doing so that you learn about clinical practice through watching her. However, she tells you about this case because it has sparked a conversation among her colleagues, and she knows that you are learning about genetic diseases and are interested in specializing in obstetrics and gynecology.

In her office, on the previous Monday, was a couple, Samantha and Édouard, who currently have a four-year-old child, Sam, with Tay-Sachs disease, an autosomal recessive disease that produces profound neurological impairment. Most children suffering from the disease die quite young. The genetic mutation responsible for this illness is most common in the Ashkenazi Jewish population. Samantha tells Dr. Miller that she is of Ashkenazi Jewish descent, and was screened for Tay-Sachs disease in a voluntary program at her college's student health service. Édouard, who is not Jewish, was only tested after Sam's diagnosis. At that time, testing confirmed that he was a Tay-Sachs carrier. He also mentioned that his father is of Cajun descent, a group also known to have an elevated frequency of the disease.

The couple wish to have another child, and they want to do so soon because they think they might be getting too old. Samantha is 36 years old and Édouard is

39. They have done some research on the internet about risks for having children with Tay-Sachs disease, and learned about a procedure known as pre-implantation genetic diagnosis (PGD), which they hope can help them avoid having another child with the disease.

Pre-implantation genetic diagnosis is an assisted reproduction procedure used to help identify genetic defects within embryos to prevent certain genetic diseases. PGD begins with the normal process of in vitro fertilization, which includes egg retrieval and fertilization in a laboratory. Over the next three days, the embryo will divide into eight cells. One or two cells are removed from the embryo and then evaluated to determine if the problematic gene is present in the embryo. In this case, an embryo that does not have the mutation in the Hex-A gene which causes Tay-Sachs will be selected for implantation. Any additional embryos that are free of the genetic mutation may be frozen for later use, while embryos with the mutated gene are destroyed. Embryos may also be kept for medical research.

Samantha and Édouard do not know much about what is involved in the process of PGD, and, when they searched online, they found a lot of conflicting information about risks and costs of the procedure as well as the moral controversy surrounding it. They personally are conflicted over their desire to have another child and they fear bringing another child into the world with Tay-Sachs. Yet, they also do not know if PGD is a reasonable option for them. They did tell Dr. Miller that they saw online that there was a major medical center that has a specialized assisted reproductive technology (ART) clinic about 30 miles away from their home.

Dr. Miller tells you that she did not have enough time to discuss the procedure with the couple and that they are coming back for a follow-up appointment next Monday. She asks you how you would advise the couple. Because she doesn't usually ask for your input, you are not sure how she will take your suggestion. You also know that she is generally quite conservative when it comes to the ethics of using technology for reproductive purposes, especially when it is not used strictly for therapeutic reasons. However, the other clinicians with whom she works are much more open to advising their patients in using reproductive technology to have children. You are not scheduled to come to shadow her that day, but you would like to be in the office when she talks to Samantha and Édouard, if they are amenable to it, and you do not have classes that day that might preclude you from coming if your preceptor would allow it.

How might you respond to your preceptor?

Background to the case

The World Health Organization defines reproductive rights as follows:

> Reproductive rights rest on the recognition of the basic right of all couples and individuals to decide freely and responsibly the number, spacing and timing of their children and to have the information and means to do so, and

> the right to attain the highest standard of sexual and reproductive health. They also include the right of all to make decisions concerning reproduction free of discrimination, coercion and violence.

In line with this definition, reproductive rights commonly include the right to legal and safe abortion; the right to birth control; freedom from coerced sterilization, abortion, and contraception; the right to access good-quality reproductive healthcare; and the right to education and access in order to make free and informed reproductive choices. As the definition and the examples attest, reproductive rights are traditionally seen as negative or liberty rights, i.e. the right not to have someone interfere, and not as a positive or entitlement right, i.e. the right for society to give a person the ability to have a child even if he or she currently cannot. Similarly, United States Supreme Court cases that established legal thinking about procreative liberty and autonomy seem to interpret reproductive rights as a right from interference. For example, *Griswold v. Connecticut* (1965) was a landmark case that affirmed the "right to marital privacy." *Eisenstadt v. Baird* (1972) extended the right of marital privacy to unmarried people, permitting them to possess contraception on the same basis as married couples. *Planned Parenthood of Southern Pennsylvania v. Casey* (1992) upheld the constitutional right to have an abortion.

However, there is a growing perception that reproduction rights consist not only of liberty rights against interference, but they are also entitlements whereby people can demand social assistance in having children. For example, currently eight states have adopted this view into law and certain fertility procedures are covered by health insurance,[19] and another seven have made it possible for fertility treatment to be covered by insurance but they have not mandated it.[20] However, even in those states that have mandated that reproduction rights are entitlement rights, the law allows for exceptions for small businesses, religious organizations and for the self-employed, and for employers who do not offer health insurance at all. The reason for these exceptions in the law is based on the negotiation of legal priorities to enable individuals to exercise their (procreative) liberty while not obstructing the (religious or economic) liberty of others.

The ambiguity in the law regarding whether reproductive rights are liberty or entitlement rights and in allowing for certain exceptions reflects the current ethical debate on the issue. The general ethical debate on the use of reproduction technology begins with a question of framing. One side frames the question in terms of individual autonomy, while the other side frames the question in terms of social responsibility. According to the frame that conceives of reproduction as a matter of individual liberty, people should have the right to produce children in any matter that they see fit. They should have the right to produce the type of children that they want, and they should be able to create any type of family that they want. The state's concern with preserving a certain image of the family does not justify prohibition of non-coital, collaborative conception. This view is also rooted in the notion that individuals have a right to choose and live the kind of life that they find meaningful and fulfilling.[21] According to the frame that conceives of reproduction as a matter of social responsibility, procreation, though seemingly a private act, has profound public meaning. It determines the relationship between one generation and the next, it shapes identities, creates attachments, and sets up responsibilities for the care and rearing of children (and the care of aging parents or other needy kin). Moreover, this view sees procreation as a way to accept, rather than reshape, engineer, or design the next generation. This view also emphasizes the idea that a child is not a possession to be created based on the parents' wishes.[22] Most people fall between these two views and recognize that, while children are not the possession of their parents, there is a natural desire to create a child that will not have as many challenges in life as he or she would without medical intervention.

In addition to the general question of how to frame the issue, the question of what to do with those embryos that are not implanted raises moral debate. The debate is similar to the debate surrounding abortion of a fetus, yet it also includes the debate as to whether the abortion analogy is applicable to unimplanted embryos or not (i.e. whether life begins at conception or pregnancy). The question of costs and equal access also influences the debate. PGD can cost up to $20,000 for the procedure itself, whether it is successful or not, and this does not include any of the other costs, such as travelling. Even if insurance covers a significant portion of the procedure's costs, individuals will still have to pay a certain portion of the expenses.

When discussing whether PGD is a viable alternative for a couple who wish to have a child, physicians should inform patients of the process of PGD so that patients can understand how their decision would be in line or contradict their moral values on the many ethical questions that PGD raises. Patients should also be aware of whether insurance will cover the costs of the procedure or not, and any other costs that may affect their decision. Undergoing PGD to have a child without Tay Sachs, when their first child suffers from the disease, may also cause feelings of guilt or other feelings. It is important for patients to be made aware that they can go to genetic counselors who can help them in their decision as well.

Case 8: Withdrawing treatment and right to die

Assignment

In this case, you will read about David, a 65-year-old man with lung cancer. David has been intubated and put on a mechanical ventilator. He wishes to be extubated, even though he knows that he will probably die as a result. You are a junior resident, and the senior resident with whom you are working is reluctant to write the order to extubate David. He also refuses to order morphine, even though hospital protocol is to administer morphine during a terminal extubation.[23] After reading the case presentation and discussion, prepare a script for your conversation with the senior resident and the nursing staff about how to proceed.

- Decisions to consider are whether the senior resident should extubate David and order the morphine or if someone else should do so, and if someone else should, who that would be.
- Please use your own personal–professional profile (or one on which your small group agrees for the purpose of this exercise) and think about how your personal–professional profile affects how you decide to proceed in this case as well as how your profile shapes the way in which you communicate that decision.
- Your action strategy should include plans for gathering the additional information you might need, identifying and approaching allies who may be helpful, recognizing and utilizing any opportunities that may be available, identifying and mitigating any challenges that you might foresee, and crafting alternative solutions that incorporate these factors.
- In preparing your script, consider not only your own perspective, but also the perspectives of the senior fellow, the nurses, David, and his family. How will the senior resident or the nurses take your suggestions? How might you be able to mitigate the tensions that have arisen among the medical team and the family? Who else might be able to help you in this endeavor? Your script should incorporate the rationalizations or responses that you anticipate from the senior resident and how you can reply to them. As such, the "script" should be more like a decision-tree than a monologue.
- Remember that the ethical question in this case is not simply what you would do yourself, but how well you, the senior resident, and the nursing staff can act on your respective values in light of the patient's goals.
- Refer to the rubric and be sure to include all elements listed when creating your script and in preparing for your explanation for why you came up with your script and action strategy.

Case presentation

David is a 65-year-old man with a history of lung cancer. His landlord found him unresponsive in his apartment and immediately called the emergency services. When they arrived, they immediately started CPR and intubated him. On arrival to the emergency room, he had a stable pulse and blood pressure, but his chest x-ray revealed white-out of his right lung and more than half of his left lung, presumably from his cancer. He was still unconscious in the emergency room and was therefore transferred to the intensive care unit for further management.

The next day, he is seen by the oncology service, who, with the ICU attending, say that the cancer has taken up so much of his lungs that he will never come off the ventilator. By the afternoon, the patient himself has woken up and indicates that he wants to be removed from the ventilator. He seems to understand his prognosis, and indicates that after his extubation, he would not want to be intubated again. He appears to have decisional capacity and is firm in his decision, and only asks that they wait until his daughters arrive.

The daughters arrive that evening, at which point he tells the nurse that they are "ready." The attendings are all gone, leaving you, a junior resident, along with the senior resident, and the nursing staff. The senior resident reluctantly writes the order to extubate him. The nurse reminds him that per hospital protocol, they will need a morphine order. The resident responds saying, "Why? I'm not killing him." The nurses press him, at which point he says, "Fine, let's get a psychiatry consult to rule out depression." Both the family and the nurses are upset at this change. The resident, though, is adamant that he does not want to be responsible for the patient's death.

Background to the case

Medical ethicists had previously distinguished between withholding and withdrawing treatment, whereby in the former the physician is passive, and, ultimately, the patient's death was caused by his or her illness. The latter, on the other hand, was seen as an act that caused harm or death. Today, many medical ethicists do not make this distinction, since in both cases, the patient will not (continue to) receive treatment and the disease will take its natural course. The American Medical Association codifies the ethical equivalence between withholding and withdrawing treatment in its Code of Medical Ethics as follows:

> While there may be an emotional difference between not initiating an intervention at all and discontinuing it later in the course of care, there is no ethical difference between withholding and withdrawing treatment. When an intervention no longer helps to achieve the patient's goals for care or desired quality of life, it is ethically appropriate for physicians to withdraw it.[24]

The justification for not distinguishing between withholding and withdrawing in secular medical ethics and law is explained through the equivalence thesis, which holds the following two premises:

1. If it would have been morally permissible to have withheld therapy (that was in fact already started), then it is now morally permissible to withdraw that therapy.
2. If, in the future, it would be morally permissible to withdraw a therapy (that has, in fact, not yet been started), then it is now morally permissible to withhold that therapy.

The equivalence thesis does not give moral weight to continuing the status quo if one is currently treating a person. Rather, the ultimate state of affairs overrides consideration of the present facts.[25] The equivalence thesis is not universally accepted by all ethicists. There are those who still consider the distinction between withholding and withdrawal as relevant, based on the difference of the medical provider's participation in removing treatment. A different way to consider the relationship of withholding and withdrawing treatment would be to consider the duty one has in continuing to treat – which is the question of whether treatment is medically effective or futile – and the degree of causation that withholding or withdrawal has in the patient's death.

In this case, however, the decision to withdraw the ventilator is not simply a medical decision, i.e. a decision as to the ventilator's efficacy in treating or maintaining the health of the patient. Rather, the patient requested its removal, even though he knows that removal of the ventilator will most likely result in his death. The right to die is an extension of the right to refuse treatment. It is not conceived to be suicide. Those who distinguish between committing suicide and refusing treatment that will result in death do so on two counts that are based on the definition of suicide. Suicide is defined as the intentional termination of one's own life. Intentionality demands that one's purpose is towards a certain goal. Moreover, the easiest way to determine one's intention is through one's actions towards that goal. When one refuses treatment, the intention or goal sought is to remove the encumbrance of medical treatment; the patient's goal is not to die. Furthermore, in refusing treatment, the patient is not terminating his or her own life; rather, death is a natural result of his or her medical condition. As such, when one refuses treatment, the patient neither intends nor terminates his or her life – in other words, he or she does not commit suicide. This is the legal as well as the predominant ethical understanding of why refusing treatment and suicide are not the same.

The use of morphine during terminal extubation is more controversial than the withholding or withdrawing treatment or simply respecting a patient's right to refuse treatment due to the fact that the physician administering it is actively alleviating pain and/or hastening the patient's death. The controversy is furthered by the fact that use of morphine is associated with concerns for the patient's comfort and the family's perceptions of the patient in pain, as well as conflicting beliefs, values, and feelings of the medical provider regarding his or her causing the death of the patient. When removing a ventilator, a patient may suffer from anticipatory distress, caused by the fears of not being able to breathe, physical discomfort from removing the ventilator and from the dyspnea (difficult or labored breathing) resulting from the removal. Also, the patient's family may perceive the patient's difficulty breathing as a sign of suffering, which may cause them distress as well. Administering morphine after a patient shows signs of distress may not be as effective as administering morphine beforehand, since physicians may not recognize the patient as suffering and the morphine may take time to become palliative. The medical provider's hesitancy to administer morphine is based on the fact that morphine will depress respiration, which may shorten the life of the patient. The question of when and how much morphine to administer during terminal extubation, therefore, is a question that requires one to balance the benefits of relieving patient suffering with the risk of shortening the patient's life.

Case 9: Determination of death

Assignment

In this case, you will read about a conflict among members of your health care team on whether to declare a patient dead based on neurological criteria or not. The family members do not believe that brain death is a valid determination of death and you are in a state that allows for either brain death and death according to cardiopulmonary criteria to be valid. After reading the case presentation and discussion, prepare a script for your conversation with your health care team on how to approach the family about what to do for the patient.

- Decisions to consider are whether to declare a patient dead based on neurological criteria or not, and how to communicate that decision to the medical team and the family. If you decide not to declare the patient brain dead, then you must consider whether, and to what extent, the medical team should continue treatment.
- Please use your own personal–professional profile (or one on which your small group agrees for the purpose of this exercise) and think about how your personal–professional profile affects how you decide to proceed in this case as well as how your profile shapes the way in which you communicate that decision.
- Your action strategy should include plans for gathering the additional information you might need, identifying and approaching allies who may be helpful, recognizing and utilizing any opportunities that may be available, identifying and mitigating any challenges that you might foresee, and crafting alternative solutions that incorporate these factors.
- In preparing your script, consider not only your own perspective, but also the perspectives of the health care team and the family. How will the various members of the team take your suggestions? How might the family? Who else might be able to help you in this endeavor? Your script should incorporate the rationalizations or responses that you anticipate from the health care team and the family and how you can reply to them. As such, the "script" should be more like a decision-tree than a monologue.
- Remember that the ethical question in this case is not simply what you would do yourself, but how well the health care team can act on their values in light of the patient's and the family's belief and values.
- Refer to the rubric and be sure to include all elements listed when creating your script and in preparing for your explanation for why you came up with your script and action strategy.

Case presentation

You are a sub-intern rotating in a medical intensive care unit in New Jersey. The patient you have been following, a 38-year-old man who suffered severe injuries to multiple organs as a result of a motorcycle accident, has been declared brain dead, but his parents, who are Evangelical Christians, state that in their church, they do not believe in brain death. They believe that death occurs only when there is an absence of a heartbeat. They want the patient to get a tracheostomy (a surgically created hole in the trachea to allow for an alternative airway to breathe) and to remain on the ventilator. The patient does not have an advanced directive, a designated health care proxy, or an organ donor card. The medical team, however, has asked the family to consider terminal extubation.[26] The patient's primary night nurse, also an Evangelical Christian, supports the family's decision, but his primary day nurse is upset at the idea of keeping his body alive. The attending, an intensivist who is in her first year of independent practice, feels it would be unethical to keep him alive because "brain dead is dead." Furthermore, you overheard the attending and the primary day nurse say that there were other patients with a higher chance of recovery that would benefit more than a dead person from the time and resources of the intensive care unit.

This conflict is making it uncomfortable for you to work as a member of the team and the patient's family is refusing to speak with any members of the team who support the brain death determination, but they continue to talk to you because you haven't shared your opinion yet.

How will you advise the team to proceed with talking to the family?

Background to the case

While brain death has become the predominant criterion for determining whether a person is dead or not, the legal and clinical guidelines for determining death and the public understanding of brain death versus other criteria of death creates controversy and sometimes conflict in the clinical setting. Before understanding how to act in a situation where different views of death are being voiced, it is important to first take a step back to see how these views were formed and the practical ramifications between them. First, there is a difference between definitions of death, criteria of death, and tests that prove that death has occurred. A definition of death is an explanation of the concept that makes its meaning explicit. Definitions of death are not explicitly scientific or medical; rather, they are social and legal. For example, two prominent definitions of death are the following:

1. Death is the permanent cessation of functioning of the organism as a whole. Despite this cessation, individual subsystems may continue to function.[27]
2. Death is the irreversible loss of that which is essentially significant to a species.

These definitions may seem to be descriptions of medical or scientific phenomena but, in truth, they are general descriptions of a state of affairs that is accepted by society or a community. On the other hand, whether this state of affairs has occurred or not is based on medical or scientific criteria and tests to confirm those criteria. In other words, providing a definition of death is a philosophical and legal task; providing criteria and selecting tests that indicate that they have been satisfied are medical tasks.

Historically, the common law in the United States gave the permanent loss of cardiopulmonary function as the criterion used to confirm the legal definition of death; however, with the increase in medical technology and the growing demand for organ donations, the law has changed to accept brain death as the primary criterion to determine death. Because definitions of death are not strictly medical or scientific, some states, which consist of populations of religious or cultural groups that do not accept the brain death criterion as valid, allow for either brain death or cardiopulmonary death criteria to be valid or will provide accommodation for those who do not accept the brain death criterion. This accommodation is meant to ensure that the constitutional right of religious freedom is protected. One such state is New Jersey. The relevant section of the New Jersey Statute states:

> 26:6A-5. Death not declared in violation of an individual's religious beliefs: The death of an individual shall not be declared upon the basis of neurological criteria pursuant to sections 3 and 4 of this act when the licensed physician authorized to declare death has reason to believe, on the basis of information in the individual's available medical records, or information provided by a member of the individual's family or any other person knowledgeable about the individual's personal religious beliefs that such a declaration would violate the personal religious beliefs of the individual. In these cases, death shall be declared, and the time of death fixed, solely upon the basis of cardio-respiratory criteria pursuant to section 2 of this act.[28]

Those states that accept a standard other than brain death as a valid criterion to determine whether death has in fact occurred, or not, do so based on the presumption that definitions of death are not strictly medical but rather incorporate philosophical or social assumptions. For example, even the philosophical justification for brain death has changed since "death based on neurological criteria" was first posited. Originally, when the Uniform Determination of Death Act (UDDA) was first proposed in 1981 as a model for states to adopt as law, cardiopulmonary criterion and neurological criterion were seen as two different but equal criteria to determine that a person has in fact died. Therefore, regardless of which criterion one used, the two criteria determined the same state of affairs. To explain, according to the cardiopulmonary criterion for death, death occurs when there is a permanent loss of cardiopulmonary function. When this criterion is met, there is permanent cessation of independent functioning of the organism as a whole. There is also an irreversible loss of that which is essentially significant to a species. The same was seen as true according to the brain death criterion, since irreversible loss of brain functioning implied loss of independent functioning for respiration and eventually heartbeat necessary to sustain life. When a person who fits the criterion of brain death is on a mechanical ventilator, it is the ventilator that is performing the respiratory function, not the person. Therefore, in line with either criterion, the person is deemed to be dead since the two parts of the function of breathing (whether the brain or the cardiopulmonary system) are intimately tied to each other.

By 2007, however, controversy still existed surrounding whether death according to neurological criterion was equivalent to death by cardiopulmonary criterion, since brain dead patients were found to still demonstrate certain integrative functions, such as normal function of the liver, kidneys, cardiovascular and endocrine systems, wound healing and fighting of infections, successful gestation of a fetus, and sexual maturation of a child, among others.[29] This led the President's Commission on Bioethics to change its position on brain death, maintaining it as a criterion for death but providing alternative philosophical support. Instead of saying that it is an equivalent criterion to cardiopulmonary death, the commission stated that a person who has lost neurological functioning to the point that it fits with the neurological criterion associated with brain death should be considered dead, since he or she has lost that which is essentially significant to the human species.

While it is important for you to think about your own values in regard to definitions and criteria of death, when communicating with patients and family members who have different beliefs than you, it is not productive to engage in philosophical debate in order to persuade others of your position. Neither is it productive simply to dismiss other's positions. In situations where there might be a conflict of values between stakeholders, communication should center on coming to consensus on how to proceed in action rather than agreement or consensus of beliefs.

If a family member believes that a patient will recover from brain death, rather than having a different definition of death based on religious or philosophical reasons, it is not a reason for religious accommodation. Giving family members hope of recovery when there is none does not help. As such, when discussing how to proceed with patients who are dead according to neurological criteria, one must be careful to be clear in communicating to a family member that, according to this criterion, the patient is determined to be in fact dead. It is not the case that the patient's brain is simply dead, while the patient is still alive. Using the term "brain dead" can be ambiguous for family members who are not familiar with the term, or who misunderstand the term to mean something other than the fact that the patient is dead. Even when communicating to family members who disagree with the neurological criterion and hold that only the cardiopulmonary criterion is valid in determining whether a person is dead or not, one should be clear that they should not think that the patient will recover.

Notes

1 *In re Tyson*, 1999 W.L. 997489.
2 www.health.ny.gov/diseases/aids/providers/testing/perinatal/breastfeeding_policy.htm
3 www.fns.usda.gov/wic/women-infants-and-children-wic
4 www.hmbana.org/about-hmbana
5 Volk, M. L., Hanson, C. V., Israel-Ballard, K., & Chantry, C. J. (2010). Inactivation of cell-associated and cell-free HIV-1 by flash-heat treatment of breast milk. *JAIDS Journal of Acquired Immune Deficiency Syndromes, 53*(5), 665–666.

6 www.ama-assn.org/delivering-care/reporting-incompetent-or-unethical-behaviors-colleagues
7 www.ama-assn.org/delivering-care/physician-responsibilities-impaired-colleagues
8 According to the American Association of Naturopathic Physicians, naturopathic medicine is "a distinct primary health care profession, emphasizing prevention, treatment, and optimal health through the use of therapeutic methods and substances that encourage individuals' inherent self-healing process." (www.naturopathic.org/content.asp?contentid=59) Naturopathy is based on the premise that people's inherent self-healing processes are ordered and intelligent. Naturopathic treatment, therefore, consists of identifying and removing obstacles to the natural healing and recovery process, as well as facilitating a person's inherent self-healing process. Naturopathy is considered a form of alternative medicine and has been condemned by allopathic medical professionals as anti-scientific and harmful to patients.
9 Low grade squamous intraepithelial neoplasia is when slightly abnormal cells are found on the surface of the cervix, and it is oftentimes caused by certain types of human papillomavirus (HPV).
10 Cervical intraepithelial neoplasia 2 is when moderately abnormal cells are found on the surface of the cervix.
11 Cervical conization refers to an excision of a cone-shaped sample of tissue from the mucous membrane of the cervix, and it is done either for diagnostic purposes or as therapy to remove pre-cancerous cells. Cervical conization does not typically affect one's ability to conceive, yet, in rare circumstances, it can lead to cervical stenosis, or a narrowing of the cervical canal, which can make it more difficult for sperm to reach their destination. Also rare, yet especially if the doctor who performs the conization is too aggressive in removing parts of the cervix, cervical conization can be associated with an increased risk of preterm delivery, miscarriage, and/or premature rupture of cervical membranes.
12 Internal validity refers to how well the design of a given research experiment can allow you to choose among alternate explanations of one's findings. If an experiment has high internal validity, then you can choose one explanation of the findings over others with a high level of confidence.
13 Impact refers to the level of change that can be attributed to a particular intervention.
14 External validity refers to how well the findings of a given research experiment applies to settings that differ from the particular setting in which the research was conducted.
15 Relying on evidence-based research studies may also be insufficient given the types of research which gets funded and published. Medical research funded by pharmaceutical and medical device companies can disproportionately influence the availability of data, since research with low economic yield but high clinical value may not get funded. Also, research on rare or orphan diseases may not get the funding necessary to establish sufficiently supported practice guidelines.
16 For example, the 1847 Code of Ethics prohibits consultation with medical practitioners who are not affiliated with the American Medical Association: "A regular medical education furnishes the only presumptive evidence of professional abilities and acquirements, and ought to be the only acknowledged right of an individual to the exercise and honors of his profession. Nevertheless, as in consultations the good of the patient is the sole object in view, and this is often dependent on personal confidence, no intelligent regular practitioner who has a license to practice for some medical board of known and acknowledged respectability, recognized by this association, and who is in good moral and professional standing in the place in which he resides, should be fastidiously excluded from fellowship, or his aid refused in consultation, when it is requested by the patient. But no one can be considered as a regular practitioner, or a fit associate in consultation, whose practice is based on an exclusive dogma, to the rejection of the accumulated experience of the profession, and of the aids actually furnished by anatomy, physiology, pathology, and organic chemistry."

17 Alternative medicine and the AMA. *The American Medical Ethics Revolution*. Baltimore: Johns Hopkins University Press, 1999, 229.
18 http://medical-malpractice.lawyers.com/professional-duty-of-care/where-is-your-doctor-when-you-need-him-most.html
19 These states are Arkansas, Massachusetts, Hawaii, Rhode Island, Illinois, Maryland, New Jersey, and Connecticut.
20 These states are California, Louisiana, Montana, New York, Ohio, Texas, and West Virginia.
21 Robertson, J. A. (1983). Procreative liberty and the control of conception, pregnancy, and childbirth, *Virginia Law Review, 69*(3), 405–464.
22 Human cloning and human dignity: An ethical inquiry. *The President's Council on Bioethics*. Washington, D.C., July 2002.
23 Terminal extubation is when the medical team withdraws mechanical ventilation from patients who are not expected to breathe independently once removed.
24 www.ama-assn.org/delivering-care/withholding-or-withdrawing-life-sustaining-treatment
25 Adapted from Bedzow, I. Why religious discourse has a place in medical ethics: An example from Jewish medical ethics. *Studies in Judaism, Humanities, and the Social Sciences, 1*(1), 107.
26 In using the term terminal extubation, there is an implication that the patient is still alive, which may cause confusion for family members when a patient is diagnosed as brain dead, since a brain dead patient would be considered dead, not alive.
27 Bernat, J. L., Culver, C. M., & Gert, B. (1981). On the definition and criterion of death. *Annals of Internal Medicine, 94*(3), 389.
28 www.braindeath.org/law/newjersey.htm.
29 Shewmon, D. A. (2001). The brain and somatic integration: insights into the standard biological rationale for equating "brain death" with death. *The Journal of Medicine and Philosophy: A Forum for Bioethics and Philosophy of Medicine, 26*(5), 457–478, Oxford University Press.

5

CONCLUSION

The need to incorporate post-decision analysis into medical ethics education is based on the following two statements:

1. In practice, ethical challenges are seldom about what one should do.
2. In practice, when faced with an ethical challenge, many people do not know how to act.

Let me explain. Many, if not all, people think it is obvious to say that it is good/right to avoid medical error and that it is good/right to stop someone from committing medical error or malpractice. Ethics debates on how to define good and bad, or right and wrong, properly, have little influence on many people's answers to these basic questions. Neither do debates on whether consequentialist or deontological moral philosophies are more appropriate when engaging in moral deliberation on what one should do when one encounters a situation of potential medical error or malpractice. Furthermore, despite the many ethical and social philosophies about the relativity of values and reasons, or whether ethics is communitarian, egoistic, or universal, many, if not most, of us not only agree with the idea that it is good/right to avoid medical error and that it is good/right to stop someone from committing medical error or malpractice, but we also believe that most other people besides ourselves share these beliefs as well.

Yet if ethical challenges are seldom about what one should do, how is it the case that, when faced with an ethical challenge, many people do not know how to act? The weakness of (medical) ethics education is that, while people learn how to think about moral questions, they are rarely taught how to act on their moral values or beliefs so as to implement their decisions successfully. In essence, ethics education spends its time thinking about what the right answer is but it does not invest in thinking about how to develop habits for acting on our values and beliefs or developing strategies for acting on them in complicated situations.

This book attempts to close the gap between moral thinking and moral acting in medical ethics situations by providing opportunities for students to develop separately the skills necessary to perform both, as well as opportunities to integrate both aspects of ethics into a mutually reinforcing set of tools. By teaching students how to think about the personal and professional values that they want to uphold, how they can communicate with others regarding the reasons for their moral decisions, and how they can implement effective action plans to carry out their decisions successfully, this book attempts to rectify the disconnect between knowing what to do and not knowing how to act. In doing so, not only will students be more effective moral and professional actors, they will also identify more strongly with the moral values they hold dear and the habits which engender those values as part of their personal and professional identity.

This latter point demonstrates the relationship between medical ethics and professionalism. Because professionalism is a value that demands that people attain certain competencies in order to express that value well, medical ethics education that promotes both ethics content and ethics skill development can be the avenue by which professionalism is introduced to students. Learning how they can rely on personal experiences as well as build on their own personal self-images to inform how they can act, and who they can be, in professional situations will allow them to appreciate the value of professionalism intrinsically and to develop into professionals who do not compartmentalize their professional behavior and their own personal moral character.

The Giving Voice to Values methodology enables this moral and professional development by shifting the ethical question from "What should you do in this situation?" to "What if you wanted to enact your values? What might you say or do?" This question shift may seem easy enough to ask, but our ability to answer these questions takes a lifelong process of growth and development. The time is ripe for medical ethics education to start asking these new questions.

Intended audience and how to use this book

This book is primarily intended as an undergraduate medical ethics textbook for pre-clerkship medical ethics courses, yet it can also be used by medical education faculty and medical students who are in their clerkships as a way to integrate ethics and professionalism education into clerkship objectives. Chapters 2 and 3, which discuss making moral decisions and acting on them, and the cases found in Chapter 4 provide both content and opportunities for students to develop milestones that are consistent with the list of educational objectives created by the Romanell Report in 2015, which discusses the role of medical ethics in achieving professionalism. Those objectives include:

1. Demonstrate an understanding of the concept of the physician as fiduciary and the historical development of medicine as a profession.
2. Recognize ethical issues that may arise in the course of patient care.
3. Utilize relevant ethics statements from professional associations to guide clinical ethical judgment and decision-making.
4. Think critically and systematically through ethical problems using bioethical principles and other tools of ethical analysis.
5. Provide a reasoned account of professionally responsible management of ethical problems and act in accordance with those judgments.
6. Articulate ethical reasoning to others coherently and respectfully.[1]

It also includes a means to assess the following performance objectives, also recommended by the Romanell Report:

1. Mastery of a basic body of medical ethics content.
2. Mastery of the intellectual skills for ethical analysis and reasoning/argument.
3. Performance in core bioethics behavioral skills: obtaining meaningful informed consent or informed refusal, assessing decision-making capacity,

breaking bad news, analyzing a case with ethics issues, and using a shared decision-making approach with patients.[2]

While this book contains content and opportunities that can be used to meet the objectives of a traditional pre-clerkship medical ethics course, *it goes above and beyond the traditional medical ethics education* to provide students with the educational tools to develop the necessary skills to deliberate and act on their own values and the values that are embedded within the professional ethos of the medical profession, to develop skills for moral action, and to close the gap between moral thinking and acting. The cases in the book also provide a means for students to learn about interprofessional collaboration and systems-based practice by asking them to consider other members of the collaborative care team and become familiar with healthcare law and various hospital policies when making moral decisions.

This book should be used as a required textbook for a medical ethics course, in conjunction with other texts and reading materials. The structure of the book is conducive to use with courses that consist of an introduction to medical ethics and a series of small group case discussion sessions. Many introductory medical ethics courses begin with a section that outlines the history of medical ethics, starting with the Hippocratic tradition through the creation of the American Medical Association's Code of Ethics to contemporary views on where the locus of medical ethics decisions lies. These courses will then provide a description of medical ethics and the difference between medical ethics and other areas of ethics. They will then provide background into how individuals make ethical decisions, focusing on the various philosophical approaches or ethical frameworks that people use. After these introductory sections, courses will then focus on particular concepts or themes, such as the patient–physician relationship, beginning-of-life and end-of-life issues, issues pertaining to medical research, and the relationships between physicians and society.

Chapter 1 of this book, which discusses ethics, professionalism, and the GVV methodology, should be assigned to complement the introductory session of a medical ethics course that reviews the history of medical ethics and the contemporary description of medical ethics. The chapter will provide context and background for the uniqueness and relevance of medical ethics for the sake of developing as a professional physician. It will also help to explain the importance of medical ethics education as part of a medical student's training in general, without compartmentalizing ethics as a distinct area of knowledge and competence.

Chapter 2 discusses the various components of making moral decisions, which include descriptions of the various ethical frameworks used in medical ethics, and should be assigned to complement the session of a medical ethics course that gives the background into how individuals make ethical decisions, focusing on the various philosophical approaches or ethical frameworks that people use. Chapter 3, which discusses how one can act on moral decisions should also be assigned at this time, since it introduces students to the idea that medical ethics entails not only thinking about ethical questions in general but in developing skills to put those decisions into effective action. While faculty may want to assign additional primary or secondary literature, these two chapters provide a concise yet thorough summary of the different factors regarding how individuals can make ethical decisions and act on them in practice, and, as such, they serve as an important supplement to the traditional focus in medical ethics education.

The cases in Chapter 4 of this book provide practical examples for many of the topics that medical ethics courses address, such as tensions in the patient–physician relationship, issues regarding beginning-of-life and end-of-life care, confidentiality, and duties to report. Also included are topics that are relevant to clinical practice and working on a healthcare team, but are not often included in traditional medical ethics courses, such as confronting a superior, speaking to colleagues about their patients' complaints, talking to members of other health care professions when conflicts on the collaborative care team arise. These additional topics are included to emphasize the point that medical ethics not only pertains to questions between patient and physician but also must recognize the interprofessionality of health care.

The cases in Chapter 4 are divided into two different types. The first set of five cases describe an ethical question and inform the students of what the protagonist wants to do in order to act on his or her values. Each case is followed by a discussion as to who the key stakeholders are and what is at stake for them, what arguments or rationalizations the protagonist is likely to encounter, and what strategies he or she can use to counter opposing arguments and/or plot a course of action for addressing the situation. The assignment for these cases is to prepare an action plan and script for the protagonist. The main pedagogical objective for these cases is for students to learn and develop skills for moral action. Because they are given the "answer" for what the protagonist wants to do, they can focus on the best ways the protagonist can implement that answer.

These cases teach students to look at the particular situations at hand, to discover organizational opportunities and hindrances, to consider personal strengths and weaknesses, and to devise action plans that can be evaluated for efficacy, without worrying about whether they are making the right choice or not. This emphasis on implementation is similar to when students learn how to perform certain medical procedures. In learning how to perform the procedures separately from learning whether they are indicated or not, students can focus fully on developing those skills required to perform the procedure properly.

Providing students with the "answer" for these cases provides an additional pedagogical benefit. The cases can allow students to practice the process of ethical deliberation without the risk of arriving at conclusions that are outside of the range of moral permissibility. When discussing moral justifications for the decision that the protagonist makes, students can consider how the "answer" can be derived from the various ethical frameworks and from ethical deliberation, rather than learning to apply those frameworks through the traditionally more open-ended approach of having students reason to an answer. The emphasis of these discussions would be on process and not conclusion, since the answer is already given; therefore, students can discuss how to think about ethical deliberation without fear that they are coming to a wrong conclusion or that ethics is relative.

This way of examining ethics cases, rather than searching for a solution, is similar to teaching high-school geometry students how to write geometric proofs. A geometric proof involves writing reasoned, logical explanations that use definitions, axioms,[3] postulates,[4] and previously proved theorems[5] to arrive at a conclusion about a geometric statement, and the practice of writing these proofs teaches students to appreciate the need for clear definitions, to evaluate evidence, and to expose the assumptions on which conclusions are based. So too, in these types of discussions, by thinking about the ethical "answer" the protagonist makes as a conclusion, students can work on defining the terms used in their deliberation, evaluate how the various factors of the moral question relate to the conclusion, and expose the assumptions on which the conclusion relies. This practice will help them develop skills for ethical deliberation when they are asked to find solutions for themselves. Of course, when engaged in this form of justificatory exercise, teachers and students must be careful not to let this type of discussion lead to the idea that ethical frameworks can be used to rationalize any answer.

In the second set of four cases, each case describes an ethical question but, for these cases, students do not prepare an action plan and script for a protagonist but rather must imagine themselves as one of the stakeholders in the case. As one of the stakeholders, their assignment is to imagine how they would want to act in the situation and to prepare a script and/or action strategy for themselves. In other words, these cases ask the student both to make a decision based on giving voice to their values and to create a plan to carry out that decision effectively. As such, it builds on the previous set of cases. By being asked to see themselves as stakeholders, these cases will show that value conflicts are natural components of interpersonal, collaborative action and that students should appreciate their own views on a matter so that they do not simply defer to consensus. At the same time, students should also become aware that effective resolution comes from engaging other stakeholders and not ignoring them.

The methodological assumption for putting these cases second is that only after students learn to appreciate what is involved in successful moral action and develop skills to do so will they incorporate these considerations into the decision-making process. By reversing the order of "decide then act" in the first set of cases by having students focus primarily on the acting part and then discussing what went into the deciding part, I hope that for the second set of cases, the students are better equipped to see the relationship between these two components, instead of seeing them as two independent points in a sequence. Moreover, once students gain experience developing action plans and scripts, they will gain confidence and actually feel that they have a real actionable choice when presented with a moral challenge, which will make it more likely for them to make ethical decisions when presented with the second set of cases.

It would be ideal for class sizes to allow students to work on cases individually, since each person could respond to the ethical question based on their own values and take into consideration their own personal–professional profile. However, oftentimes class sizes do not allow for so many students to present their action strategies and presentations individually in the time allotted for class sessions. Therefore, the small group session formats below suppose that students will have to work in groups for their cases and presentations. If class sizes allow it, I strongly recommend that students prepare their own scripts and strategies, even if they discuss ideas and possible solutions with their fellow students.

For small group sessions that ask students to work on the first five cases, one potential format for the session would be as follows: Before the session begins, students should read the case, be able to state what the protagonist wants to do and make note of the various factors relayed in the case presentation that might affect the protagonist's ability to act on that decision. Students should also begin to think of the protagonist's personal–professional profile, and how that profile influences the types of actions the protagonist might be more or less willing to do. Depending on the class size, at the beginning of the class, students should be grouped into smaller units, in order to work on the assignment for the case. Before working on the action plan and script, however, they should first go through the discussion section together to make sure that each member of the group understands the various factors involved that must be considered and agree to a personal–professional profile for the protagonist. Students should be able to use outside materials that they may need to help them create their action strategies, since many of the cases require knowledge of laws or hospital policies relevant to the case or the scopes of practice and roles of other health care professionals that they may choose to include in their action plan. While students are working on their assignment, teachers should make themselves available to the students to answer questions or provide guidance. Teachers should be cognizant, however, that the assignment is student directed, and, therefore, teachers should allow students the opportunity to create action plans and scripts on their own. After the smaller student groups have created their action plans and scripts, each student group should select one to two students to present the group's script and action strategy, where the selected students role play their scripts in front of the other students in the class.[6] This is not an "adversarial role play," but rather a presentation of the group's script, which will typically be more than just a single "conversation." Rather, it will be more similar to a decision tree. You can see an example of this in Appendix II. Another one to two students should then explain how they came up with the script and action strategy. This explanation does not need to be a play-by-play of the group's working through their process. Rather, it should include explanation of how the protagonist's personal–professional profile informed their action plan, and how their action plan identified information needed, approached various stakeholders, recognized opportunities and/or challenges, and crafted alternative solutions.

After each presentation, the students from the other group(s) should discuss their scripts and strategies with the presenter(s), with a primary focus on the details of the communication and the steps of the action plan itself. The other students should take the lead in discussing the way the script imagined how the presenter(s) should speak to other members of the team, made assumptions in anticipating responses, how the plan responded to potential rationalizations, and whether there were other ways to act that may be more effective. By doing so, students work together to reflect on the script and action plan to gain (vicarious) experience for the future. Teachers should highlight the assumptions students made in creating the script and action plan and add guidance and insight when appropriate. They should also keep the conversation moving in a productive way. This will allow students to think about their own action strategies, as well as reflect on other students' views.

For these five cases, the session should end with a facilitator-led discussion on how the protagonist's decision can be shown to be a proper moral choice by having students define the terms or concepts used in the scenario, evaluate how the various factors of the moral question relate to the protagonist's decision, and discuss the moral and legal assumptions on which the conclusion relies. This ethical discussion can conclude with the teacher providing broader instruction on the medical ethics concepts that pertain to the case.

For small group sessions that ask students to work on the second set of four cases, one potential format for the session would be as follows: Before the session begins, students should read the case and think about how they would decide to act. Teachers may want to assign relevant readings, such as position papers, applicable laws, regulations, or hospital policies, or articles that can inform students about some of the concepts related to the case. If teachers do not assign additional readings, students should be informed that they might need to do research on their own in order to appreciate the professional, interprofessional, organizational, or legal aspects that might inform their decision and action plan. Depending on the class size, at the beginning of the class, students should be grouped into smaller units, in order to work on the assignment for the case. Students may be grouped by their gut reactions, though it is not necessary to divide the class in this way. However, depending on the case and the experience level of the students, it may be helpful to have students initially grouped by their gut reactions, so that students who have similar inclinations can work together to examine the rationality and persuasiveness of their own reactions. If students are not grouped by their gut reactions and have to consider at the outset both their own biases and those with whom they disagree, it may be more difficult to work through to a decision, since the group might get caught up reflecting on why each person had a different gut response. Students should not be grouped so that each group takes opposing positions in order for the class to "get to see all sides." Making students take a position that is not in line with their own values is, in fact, more detrimental than helpful, because it causes students to think that ethics is simply relative and rhetorical without there being better or worse decisions for ethical questions. Because, for the cases in this book, medical law and hospital or professional policies are pretty clear as to what a professional should do generally in these situations, the positions that the students' action plans and scripts take should be assessed based on their compliance with medico-legal and medical ethics norms. This will ensure that students are not practicing ways to act that are clearly out of step with the basic boundaries of professional behavior. In other words, ethics codes and regulations provide norms which speak to general circumstances, but they leave a lot of room for individuals to determine for themselves how they should act in particular situations so that their actions are appropriate. As such, the ethical directives of medical law and ethics should serve to set the boundaries of what should not be done, but they do not prescribe what individuals can, and should do, in any particular instance. The variability of the students' action plans and scripts will thus stem from how each student can fulfill the general guidelines of what to do given the particularities of the case and given their own personal–professional profiles and their own values.

After the smaller student groups have reached a decision and created their action plans and scripts, each student group should select one to two students to present the group's script and action strategy, where the selected students role play their scripts in front of the other students in the class.[7] Again, just like with the first set of cases, this is not an "adversarial role play," but rather a presentation of the group's script, which will typically be more than just a single "conversation." Rather, it will be more similar to a decision tree. Another one to two students should then explain how they came up their decision, discussing both the ethical reasoning for their decision and the strategy decisions for their script and action plan.

After each presentation, the other students in the class should discuss the reasoning processes and strategies with the presenting group. Teachers should also participate and add guidance and insight when appropriate, keeping the conversation moving in a productive way. The session should end with a teacher-led discussion on how the topics inherent to the case inform medical ethics more generally as well as how they can inform other challenges that students may confront in the future.

Student scripts and explanations of their action strategies can be assessed using the rubric below. The rubric is primarily meant for formative, narrative assessment of students. Formative assessment refers to the type of assessment that guides future learning by providing reassurance, promoting reflection, and shaping values. It is different from summative assessments, which are intended to make an overall judgment about competence.[8] One of the purposes of the formative assessment rubric should be to provide students with concrete comments to help them reflect on their scripts and action plans in a way that allows them to develop and integrate faculty insights into later action. As such, Jenny Rudolph et al. state "Formative assessment 'forms' trainees in two ways: 1) it shapes skills and knowledge through feedback, and 2) it helps develop professional identity through the social interaction of learning conversations."[9] Narrative assessment can allow formative assessment to take part as an active conversation between faculty and students, so that students are not only aware of how they might have met expectations or not, but how they might be able to improve in the future.

Student groups should be assessed after each session so that they receive continual feedback on their progress, with the goals of identifying students' strengths and weaknesses, guiding students' development of decision-making and action skills, and supporting their intrinsic motivation to acquire knowledge and skill in medical ethics and professional identity formation.[10] Before the course begins, students should be given the assessment rubric so that they know what they should be trying to achieve with their scripts and action strategies (by looking at the column describing what will be assessed). The rubric will thus also serve as an ideal benchmark for what students should expect of themselves when faced with having to make an ethical and professional decision.

TABLE A1.1

SCRIPT AND ACTION PLAN ASSESSMENT RUBRIC		
	N/A	**Comment**
Describes protagonist's/one's own personal–professional profile		
Answered questions of personal purpose.		
Answered questions of risk.		
Answered questions of personal communication style and preference.		
Answered questions of loyalty.		
Answered questions of self-image.		
Ethical decision		
Demonstrated awareness of biases' effect on gut reactions.		
Identified salient facts and values.		
Reached a decision based on an explicit value(s).		
Applied ethical frameworks to examine decision.		
Demonstrated reflection as to how decision demonstrates held value(s).		
Action strategy		
Demonstrates relationship between strategy and profile.		
Identified additional information needed.		
Identified and approaches various stakeholder.		
Recognized and utilizes opportunities.		
Recognized and mitigates challenges.		
Crafted alternative solutions.		
Script		
Made clear protagonist's/one's own view.		
Anticipated and responded to potential rationalizations.		
Offered solution(s) with clear plan of execution.		
Script was logical or structured.		
Script did not contain ambiguous words and inappropriate medical jargon.		

Notes

1 Carrese, J. A., Malek, J., Watson, K., Lehmann, L. S., Green, M. J., McCullough, L. B., ... & Doukas, D. J. (2015). The essential role of medical ethics education in achieving professionalism: The Romanell Report. *Academic Medicine, 90*(6), 744–752.
2 Ibid.
3 Axioms are self-evident truths or the basic facts that are accepted without any proof.
4 Postulates are statements that are assumed to be true without proof.
5 Theorems are statements that can be proved to be true.
6 Teachers may decide to assign the first part of the class session, where the smaller groups come up with their action plans and scripts, as class preparation and begin each class immediately with the groups' action plan and script presentations.
7 Teachers may decide to assign the first part of the class session, where the smaller groups come up with their action plans and scripts, as class preparation and begin each class immediately with the groups' action plan and script presentations.
8 Epstein, R. M. (2007). Assessment in medical education. *The New England Journal of Medicine, 2007*(356), 387–396.
9 Rudolph, J. W., Simon, R., Raemer, D. B., & Eppich, W. J. (2008). Debriefing as formative assessment: closing performance gaps in medical education. *Academic Emergency Medicine, 15*(11), 1011.
10 Abu-Zaid, A. (2013). Formative assessments in medical education: A medical graduate's perspective. *Perspectives on Medical Education, 2*(5–6), 358–359.

Example action plan and script for Case 1

This action plan and script is based on what faculty could expect from first- or second-year medical students, based on their level of personal experience and their experience working in healthcare.

Maria's personal–professional profile

"In order to make this case as relevant for me as possible, I will assume that Maria's personal–professional profile is similar to my own."[1]

Maria's personal and professional goals are to enjoy the work that she does every day and to have that work provide her with financial security. Maria personally enjoys helping people and experiencing the appreciation that she receives from the people that she helps. She does not define herself by her job, but she does see her job as a way to express her own beliefs and values in the world. As such, she could not act one way at work and another way outside of work. While Maria gets excited about the intellectual aspects of the job, in terms of learning new skills and encountering complex medical problems, she is most passionate about the social impact she makes on people, whether that be in improving her patients' quality of life or even in making the people with whom she works smile more. She sees her personal and professional impact on the world in terms of how many lives she can improve, and she sees her professional ambition being tied to her ability for impact.

Maria is a risk taker when she feels that she is doing what she believes is right, since she sees the consequences of doing something she believes is wrong as much worse than any other consequence. However, she is very risk averse in terms of taking chances with low probabilities of success. As such, there are times when she will do what she believes she must but in a way that is less effective because of her fear of stepping out of her comfort-zone. However, she realizes that chance favors the prepared, and she tries to be as prepared as she can be so as to take bigger chances while mitigating risk.

As a second-year resident, she realizes that she is very dependent on her superiors for her advancement and professional success, and will do whatever she can to defer to them when it does not go against her own beliefs and values. She is not friends with the fellow or the attending, but she has become friendly with the other residents and the nursing staff.

Given her feeling that she is dependent on her superiors, yet also that she cannot just follow their lead if it goes against what she stands for, Maria feels torn about how to confront the fellow, not whether she should or not. Because she sees herself as personally loyal to her patients and to her sense of self, even when professionally she tries to be loyal to her superiors for the sake of her own development and advancement, her idealism is combined with a bit of pragmatism. She knows that she would never openly contradict a superior but would always try to communicate her position through questions. She also knows that, generally, it is easier to get the answer she wants when all the preparatory work is already in place, so she generally does whatever she can do to bring her decision to action even as she is still asking for permission to do it. She feels that she can always undo her preparatory work if she doesn't get the permission for which she is hoping, but she doesn't want lack of time or the feeling that something requires too much effort to be a reason not to get what she wants.

Maria's action strategy and script

Given her personal–professional profile, Maria orders the local anesthetic at the same time that she orders the chest tube. Though this act is risky because it can be interpreted by the fellow to be in direct contradiction to what she told her, Maria is prepared to tell the fellow, if she is asked, that, as she was ordering the chest tube, she was told that the hospital usually also applies a local anesthetic to the area before inserting the tube. She thinks that by using the passive voice, she would not have to single out the nurse with whom she spoke in case the fellow got angry. Also, by saying that the hospital usually applies a local anesthetic, she would be saying what is customary without going into whether it is official hospital policy or not, so as not to directly contradict what the fellow said. In any event, Maria hopes that she can speak to the fellow about the local anesthetic before the fellow even asks about why she ordered it.

In speaking to the fellow, Maria has three primary objectives: First, she wants to make sure that she can apply the local anesthetic so as not to cause unnecessary pain to the infant. Second, she wants to have the fellow tell her to apply the local anesthetic, rather than demand from the fellow that she do so. Her desire to have the fellow tell her to do it, rather than demanding to do it outright, is based on her discomfort contradicting the fellow. She fears that contradicting the fellow might strain her relationship with her and make it less likely in the future to gain experience working with her. If, however, she is unable to ask the fellow questions in a way that gets her to change her mind, or if, during the conversation she sees that asking the fellow outright would not strain their professional relationship, then Maria would say directly that she intends to apply the local anesthetic (see paragraph #9 of the conversation tree that follows). This choice is based on the fact that while she is deferential to authority, she sees the consequences of doing something she believes is wrong as much worse than any other consequence. Third, Maria wants to learn if, or how, the medical team must inform the parents and get consent from them to insert the chest tube.

Script

The script is not simply a written dialogue, but rather more similar to a decision tree. Therefore, each subsequent statement by Maria depends on how the fellow responds to her previous question or remark. Also, it is possible to combine Maria's different responses if the conversation allows it and it serves Maria's benefit. It is also possible that the conversation with the fellow will ultimately include different questions or comments, or take a turn that does not directly reflect the statements below. As such, the different steps of the dialogue are simply preparatory remarks and could be adapted when the conversation occurs. These preparatory remarks, however, do encompass what I foresee could probably occur.

Immediately after ordering the supplies, but before doing the procedure, Maria would go to the fellow and speak to her privately with the following potential script:

1. **Maria**: "Because I am still gaining experience inserting a chest tube, do you mind if I ask you a few questions about how to handle the procedure and about notifying the parents about it?"

   a **Fellow**: "Sure."

2. **Maria**: "Thanks. When I went to order the chest tube, the question of applying a local anesthetic came up, and I was told that it is customary. I also remember learning how pain in pediatrics might be different than in adults but not by much. Have you seen a big difference between pain thresholds for adults and children?"

   a **Fellow**: "Yea, actually, let's apply the local anesthetic. Make sure that you order it as well."

   b **Fellow**: "Not really. In this case, applying a local anesthetic could go either way."

   c **Fellow**: "There isn't a big difference, but the insertion should be quick and relatively painless if you do it correctly."

3. **Fellow**: "Not really. In this case, applying a local anesthetic could go either way."

a **Maria**: "If it could go either way, and I need the practice, could I also apply the local anesthetic? It wouldn't be out of what is customary, and it could help the baby with the pain."

1. **Fellow**: "Sure, go ahead."
2. **Fellow**: "You don't need practice applying local anesthetic. It's not that hard."

4. **Fellow**: "You don't need practice applying local anesthetic. It's not that hard."

a **Maria**: "The practice wouldn't necessarily be in applying the local anesthetic alone. It would be more about doing the procedure, including applying the anesthetic and then inserting the chest tube. I know it might not be that hard, but it's more about creating the routine of it than developing skills for the separate steps."

5. **Fellow**: "There isn't a big difference, but the insertion should be quick and relatively painless if you do it correctly."

a **Maria**: "Well, I am still practicing my technique, and while I am confident that I could do it, applying the local anesthetic might make it easier for me, since I could focus on the insertion without being nervous that I might hurt the patient. Would it be okay to apply the local anesthetic?"

6. **Maria**: "Also, when we talk to the parents about inserting the chest tube, how should we bring up the topic of the local anesthetic?"

a **Fellow**: "Why would we bring it up?"
b **Fellow**: "While we need to obtain consent to insert the chest tube, it won't be that difficult, since it is in the child's best interest to do it. We would just tell them we are doing it in order to remove the air accumulated between their child's lungs and chest wall, to make it easier for him to breathe. We don't need really to bring up all the details as to how we are doing it."

7. **Fellow**: "Why would we bring it up?"

a **Maria**: "Well, they might ask if it hurts or not. And, even if they don't, if it is customary to apply local anesthetic before inserting the chest tube and we don't do it, I would be afraid they may question our care. My assumption is that the parents would ask for the local anesthetic even if the benefits were marginal in order to lessen any potential pain to their child."

8. **Fellow**: "While we need to obtain consent to insert the chest tube, it won't be that difficult, since it is in the child's best interest to do it. We would just tell them we are doing it in order to remove the air accumulated between

their child's lungs and chest wall, to make it easier for him to breathe. We don't need really to bring up all the details as to how we are doing it."

a **Maria**: "Even if they will go along with our recommendation to insert the chest tube, they have been worrying and have stayed around their baby since he got here. Couldn't we inform them in a way that keeps them in the loop of what we are doing and makes them feel involved in the care of their baby? They wouldn't say no to the insertion and it would show them that we are not ignoring them. I am afraid that if we don't make them feel included in the decision-making process, they might feel that we are not taking care of their child properly."

Maria should then find a way to introduce the comment 7a.

9. **Maria**: I really don't feel comfortable inserting the chest tube without first applying the local anesthetic. I know that you said it wasn't necessary, but it seems to be customary at the hospital, and, for my own sake, I couldn't just insert the tube without first lessening any potential pain the infant would experience by my doing so. It wouldn't take much time to apply the anesthetic, it won't negatively affect the infant's care, it will show the parents that we care for their child, and it would help me do the procedure. If you don't mind, if I am going to insert the chest tube, I am going to apply the local anesthetic first. (The forcefulness of this statement is based on the assumption that this is a "worst case" situation. If Maria can express her desire to apply the local anesthetic in a milder tone, then she would choose to do so. She is, nevertheless, prepared to be forceful if she needs to be.)

Note

1 It would be good for students to take such a stance in creating a protagonist's personal–professional profile, but it is not necessary. If they choose to create a profile that is different from their own, they can also learn the value of understanding another person's strengths and preferences.

For Product Safety Concerns and Information please contact our EU representative GPSR@taylorandfrancis.com Taylor & Francis Verlag GmbH, Kaufingerstraße 24, 80331 München, Germany